The Ultimate Beginner Series®

KEYBOARD COMPLETE

Debbie Cavalier • Larry Steelman • Henry Brewer • David Garfield

INTRODUCTION

The keyboard is one of the most enjoyable instruments you can play. With this book and DVD, you will learn all the basics you need to start playing and have a solid foundation that will enable you to play blues and rock.

The Basics section will get you started by teaching about body and hand positions, how to read music, how to play chords and scales, and even the basics of improvisation.

The Blues section teaches you the basics of playing the blues. Topics include the 12-bar blues progression, triplet feel, blues licks, blues soloing, and more.

The Rock section gives you everything you need to play rock. You will explore how to create chord voicings, rock improvisation, the shuffle feel, scales, and rock licks. There are also tips on playing in a band.

Also included are play-along tracks featuring legendary recording artists that will enable you to instantly apply the new rhythms, techniques, and licks to music.

Let's dig in and get started playing the keyboard.

The included DVD contains MP3 audio files of every example in the book. Use the MP3s to ensure you're capturing the feel of the examples and interpreting the rhythms correctly.

To access the MP3s on the DVD, place the DVD in your computer's DVD-ROM drive. In Windows, double-click on My Computer, then right-click on the DVD drive icon. Select Explore, then double-click on the DVD-ROM Materials folder. For Mac, double-click on the DVD icon on your desktop, then double-click on the DVD-ROM Materials folder.

Alfred Publishing Co., Inc.
16320 Roscoe Blvd., Suite 100
P.O. Box 10003
Van Nuys, CA 91410-0003
alfred.com

Book and DVD (with case)
ISBN-10: 0-7390-5612-3
ISBN-13: 978-0-7390-5612-7

Book and DVD (without case)
ISBN-10: 0-7390-5613-1
ISBN-13: 978-0-7390-5613-4

Cover photographs:
Blue energy © istockphoto.com/Raycat

CONTENTS

BASIC KEYBOARD

Hand and Body Position 5

The Piano Keyboard 6

Reading Rhythm Notation 7

Reading Music Notation...8

Right Hand Chords 9

Left Hand Chords 11

Playin' the Blues 14

Major Scales 25

Minor Scales..33

BLUES KEYBOARD

Review: Chords 41

12-Bar Progression 43

Shuffle Blues 45

Triplet Feel 55

Shuffle Boogie..63

The Turnaround...64

Blues Endings 68

Blues Soloing 70

Blues Licks...72

ROCK KEYBOARD

The Blues..76

Chord Voicings..80

Sounds and Parts...82

Improvising...89

Scales, Modes and Chords...93

Playing in a Band...106

SCALE CHARTS

Major Scales..107

Minor Scales..108

Blues Scales..109

Major Pentatonic Scales..110

Mixolydian Modes...111

Dorian Modes...112

CONTENTS

BASIC KEYBOARD

Hand Position

As you sit at the keyboard, place the palms of each hand on your knees. Your fingers will assume a curved position. Keep this hand position as you gently place your fingers on the keyboard.

Shaping The Fingers

Gently hold your fingers in a curved shape. Your wrists should be relaxed and level with your forearms.

Left Hand and Right Hand Finger Numbers

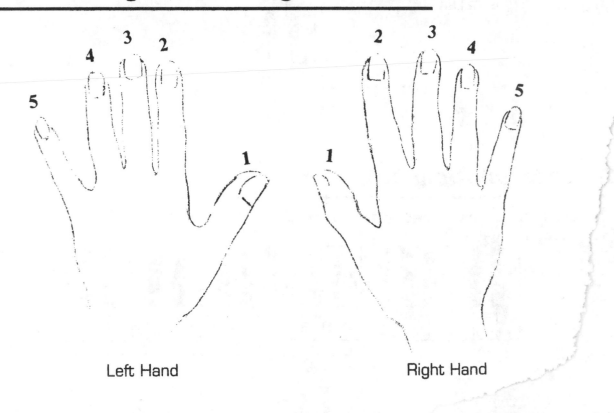

Left Hand   Right Hand

THE PIANO KEYBOARD

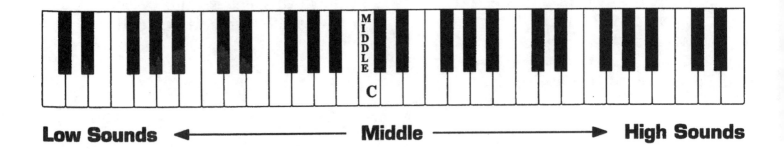

Low Sounds ◄———————— **Middle** ————————► **High Sounds**

Black Keys

The piano keyboard has black keys and white keys.

The black keys are divided into groups of two  and three.

Finding C

The note to the left of the two black keys (just below) is called C.

The Musical Alphabet

Notes are named for the first seven letters of the alphabet, A–G.

One Octave

7

READING RHYTHM NOTATION

The duration of musical sounds (long or short) is indicated by different types of notes.

WHOLE NOTE   HALF NOTE   QUARTER NOTE

Music is divided into equal parts called MEASURES or BARS.
BAR LINES indicate the beginning and end of measures.
DOUBLE BAR LINES, one thin and one thick, show the end of a piece.

TIME SIGNATURES placed at the beginning of a piece of music show the number of beats (or counts) in each measure and the kind of note that receives one beat.

$\frac{4}{4}$ means four beats in each measure.   In $\frac{4}{4}$ time: a whole note ○ receives 4 beats

$\frac{4}{4}$ means a quarter note (♩) gets one beat.   a half note receives 2 beats

a quarter note receives 1 beat

Eighth Notes

One eighth note looks like a quarter note with a flag added to its stem. ♪ or ♩

Groups of two or four eighth notes are joined by a beam.

Two eighth notes equal one quarter note.

Four eighth notes equal one half note.

Eight eighth notes equal one whole note.

In $\frac{4}{4}$ time an eighth note receives 1/2 a beat. $\frac{4}{4}$ 1 & 2 & 3 & 4 &

Eighth Note Triplets

An eighth note triplet fills the time of one quarter note.

Ties

A tie connects two notes of the same pitch. The two notes are held as if they are one. $\frac{4}{4}$ 1 2 3 4 | 1 2 3 4

READING MUSIC NOTATION

The Music Staff

Music is written on a five line staff.
Between each line there is a space.
There are four spaces on a staff.

Line 5	
	Space 4
Line 4	
	Space 3
Line 3	
	Space 2
Line 2	
	Space 1
Line 1	

Musical sounds are shown by the position of notes on the staff. Notes on the higher lines and spaces sound higher than those on the lower ones.

At the beginning of each staff there is a clef. The treble clef looks like this:

Treble clef:

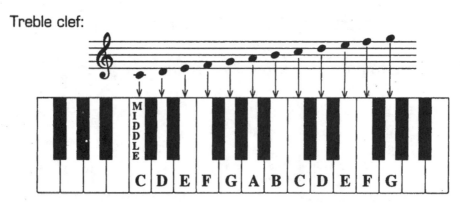

The bass clef looks like this:

Bass clef:

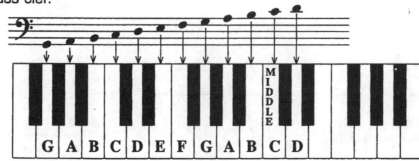

RIGHT HAND CHORDS

Musical Alphabet — Find middle C with your right hand and play the musical alphabet one octave from C to C.

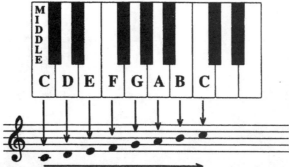

Example 1: C Chord

Chords are made up of three or more notes played simultaneously. The C chord is made of the notes C, E, G. It is called the I chord because it is built on the first scale step in the key of C. Use the thumb to play C, the 2nd finger to play E and the 4th finger to play G.

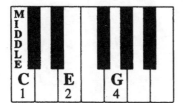

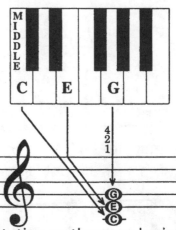

Chords can be written on a music staff using notation or they can be indicated in the form of a letter called a chord symbol which is located above the staff. The exercises in this book use both.

Play the C chords in the exercise below.

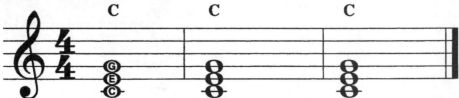

Moveable Chords

Using the same chord shape, build chords on any of the scale steps. Use your right hand thumb as your reference point. Start with C, move up to D, then to E, etc. Remember to keep the chord shape the same and use your thumb as a reference point.

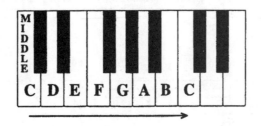

Example 2: F Chord

The F chord is made of the notes F, A, and C. It is called the IV chord because it is built on the fourth scale step in the key of C.

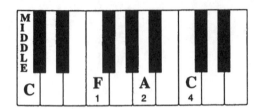 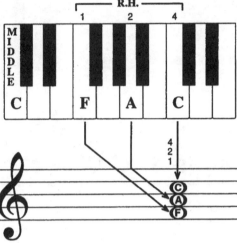

Try moving from the C chord to the F chord and back to C.

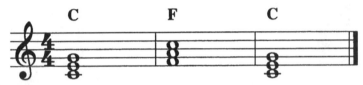

Example 3: G Chord

The G chord is made of the notes G, B, and D. It is called the V chord because it is built on the fifth scale step in the key of C.

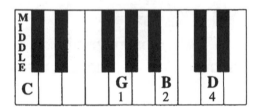 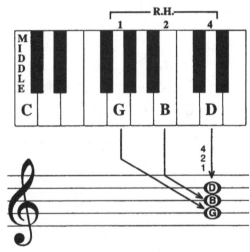

Example 4: Chord Progressions

Play the chord progressions listed below.

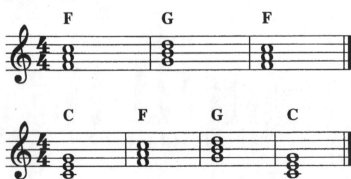

LEFT HAND CHORDS

Musical Alphabet (backwards) — Find middle C with your left hand and play the musical alphabet backwards one octave from C to C.

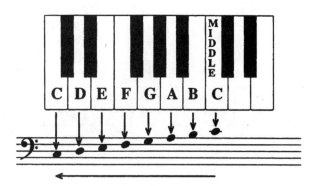

Example 5: C Chord – Left Hand

Using your left hand, put your 5th finger on C (below middle C) and your 1st finger on G. Play these notes together.

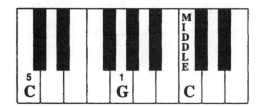

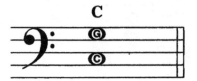

Example 6: F Chord – Left Hand

Keep your left hand in the same shape and move your 5th finger up to F and your 1st finger on middle C. Use your 5th finger (or pinky) as your reference point.

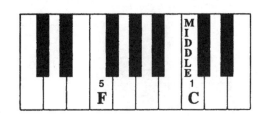

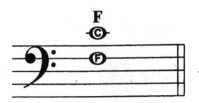

Example 7: Chord Progressions

Try moving between C and F chord positions with your left hand. Remember to use your pinky as your guide.

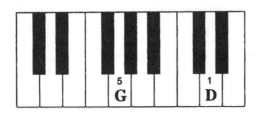

Example 8: G Chord – Left Hand

Using the same hand shape, try the G chord position.

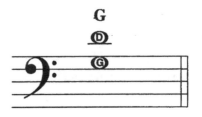

Example 9: Chord Progressions

Play the left hand F and G positions as written below.

Play the left hand C, F and G positions as written below.

Example 10: Chords – Hands Together

When putting the hands together, it's important to utilize the skills you learned earlier using your hands separately. Target the right hand with the thumb and the left hand with the pinky.

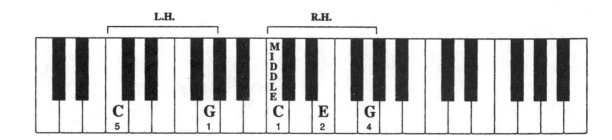

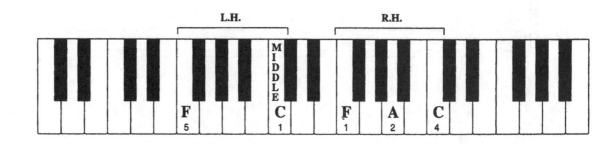

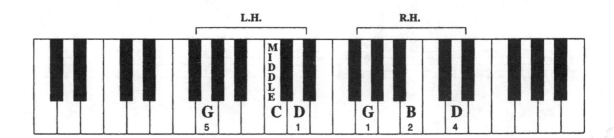

Example 11: Chord Progressions

Try the chord progression below with hands together.

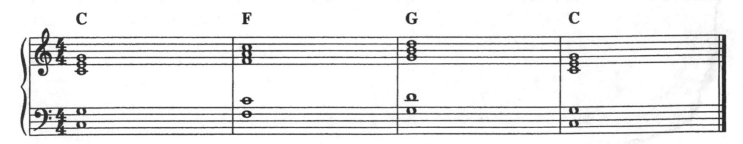

PLAYIN' THE BLUES

Example 12

The three chords learned so far form the basis for the Blues progression. Hold each chord for 4 counts.

The Blues

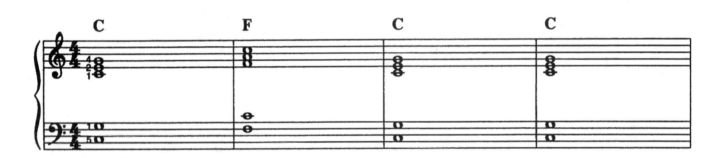

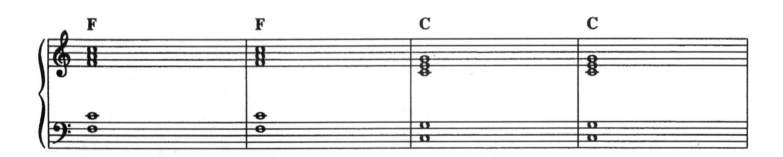

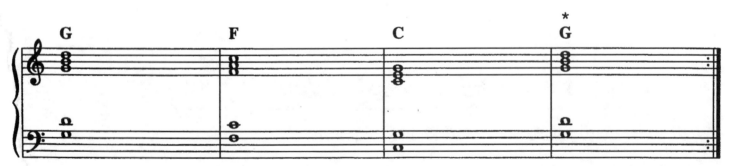

*Last time end on a C chord.

:‖ is a repeat sign. Go back to the beginning and play the song again.

BLUES VARIATION - RIGHT HAND ALTERNATING PATTERNS

Now we will "dress up" the chords in the blues progression a little to sound more like the blues players you may hear on recordings. Try these patterns at a slow tempo and gradually increase your speed until you can play with the blues recording on page 13.

Example 13: C Chord

Move from fingers 2 and 4 on E and G to fingers 3 and 5 on F and A. Alternate with the 1 finger on C.

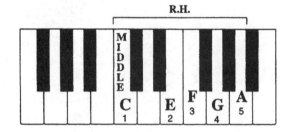

Example 14: F Chord

Move from fingers 2 and 4 on A and C to fingers 3 and 5 on B♭ and D. Alternate with the 1 finger on F.

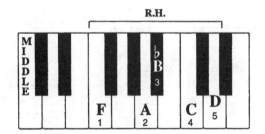

Practice moving between the C and F right hand chord variations as shown below.

---

*An ACCIDENTAL is a flat (♭), sharp (♯), or natural (♮). A flat sign (♭) in front of a note means to play the very next key lower. A sharp sign (♯) in front of a note means to play the very next key higher. Accidentals affect all following notes of that pitch within the measure. A natural (♮) cancels a sharp or flat.

Example 15: G Chord

Move from fingers 2 and 4 on B and D to fingers 3 and 5 on C and E. Alternate with the 1 finger on G.

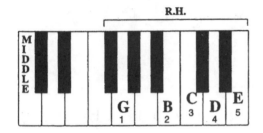

Example 16: Chord Progressions

Practice moving between the G and F chord variations as shown below.

Practice moving between the C, F and G chord variations as shown below.

BLUES VARIATION – LEFT HAND ALTERNATING PATTERNS

Example 17: C Chord

Put the left hand 5th finger on C (below middle C) and the 1st finger on G. Move the 1st finger from G up to A and back to G while playing C with finger 5.

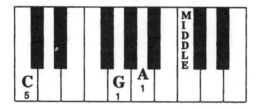

Example 18: F Chord

Put the left hand 5th finger on F and the 1st finger on C. Move the 1st finger from C up to D and back to C while playing F with finger 5.

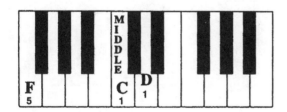

Practice moving between the C and F chord left hand variations as shown below.

Example 19: G Chord

Put the left hand 5th finger on G and the 1st finger on D. Move the 1st finger from D up to E and back to D while playing G with finger 5.

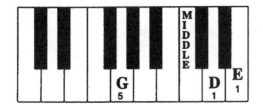

Practice moving between the G and F chords left hand variations as shown below.

Practice moving between the C, F and G chord left hand variations as shown below.

CHORD VARIATIONS – HANDS TOGETHER

Example 20: C Chord

Play the C Blues variation chords with the hands together.

 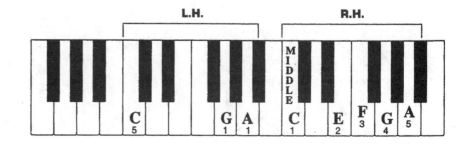

Example 21: F Chord

Play the F Blues variation chords with the hands together.

 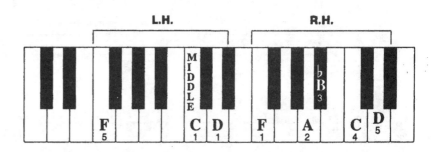

Try alternating between the C and F Blues variation chords with the hands together.

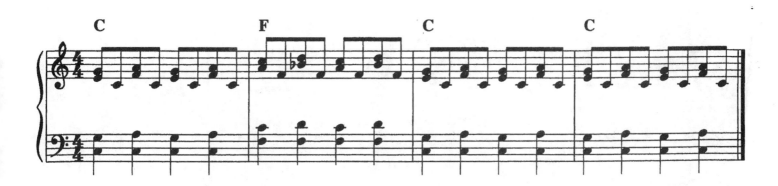

20

Example 22: G Chord

Play the G Blues variation chords with the hands together.

 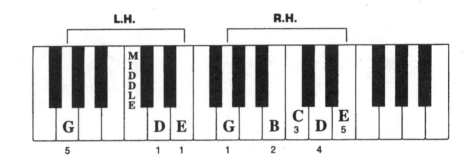

Try alternating between the G and F Blues variation chords with the hands together.

Try alternating between the C, F, and G Blues variation chords with the hands together.

Example 23

Utilizing the chord variations learned so far, play the Blues progression written below.

BLUES VARIATION

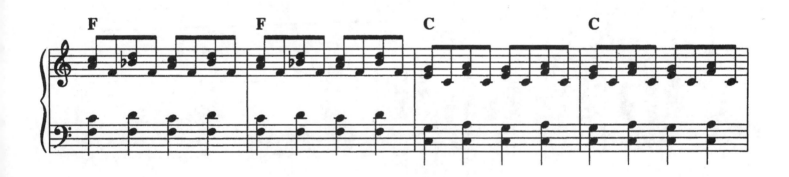

*Last time end on a C chord.

Example 24: Arpeggios

Arpeggios are chords played one note at a time. The left hand plays the root of the chord followed by the right hand which plays the notes of the chord, one at a time.

C Arpeggio (major)

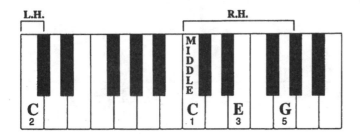 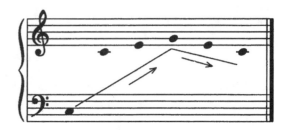

A Arpeggio (minor)

Move the same pattern for C down 2 scale steps to A. Use the left hand 4th finger to play the root of the chord.

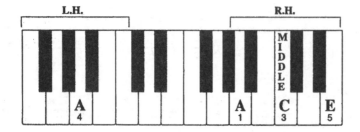 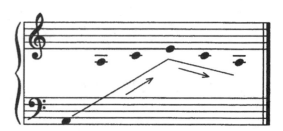

Major and Minor

The C triad in the key of C is a major triad. The A triad in the key of C is called a minor triad. It has a sadder, darker sound. Minor chord symbols are notated with a lower case m. (Am)

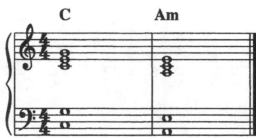

Dm Arpeggio

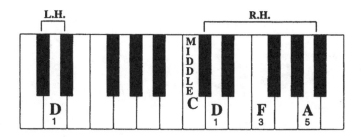 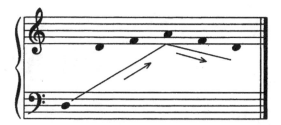

G Arpeggio

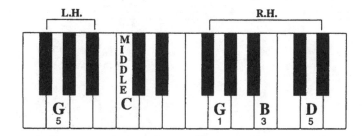 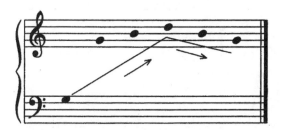

Example 25: Putting It All Together

The arpeggios below are notated in eighth note triplets to match the rhythmic performance of the recording. See page 6 for triplet information.

Arpeggio Progression

Example 26

ARPEGGIO BALLAD

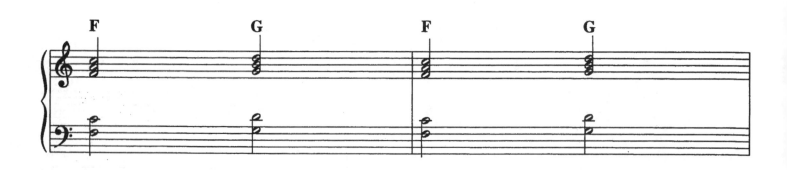

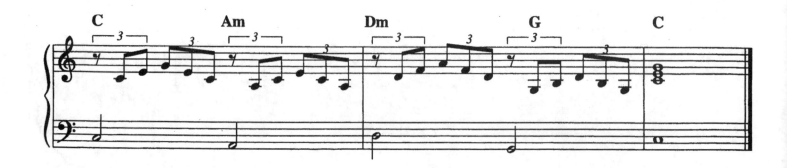

MAJOR SCALES

Example 27: C Major Scale

Earlier in this book you learned the musical alphabet from C to C. These 8 notes are also called the C major scale.

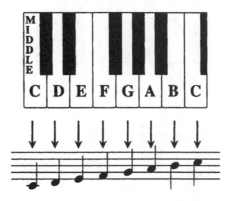

C Major Scale – Ascending

There is a standard fingering technique used to play the C major scale. Start with the thumb. After you play the 3rd finger, cross under with your thumb to get to the 4th step. Try to make this transition as smooth as possible.

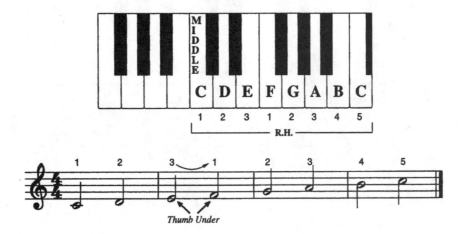

C Major Scale – Descending

Now try the C major scale descending. Play the same notes and fingerings in reverse order.

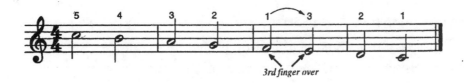

C Major Scale Ascending and Descending

Try playing the C major scale ascending and descending.

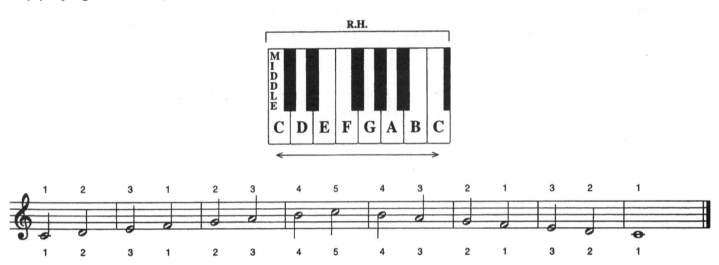

C Major Scale Ascending and Descending – 2 Octaves

A cross-over between the 7th and 8th scale degrees is needed to play a 2 octave C major scale.

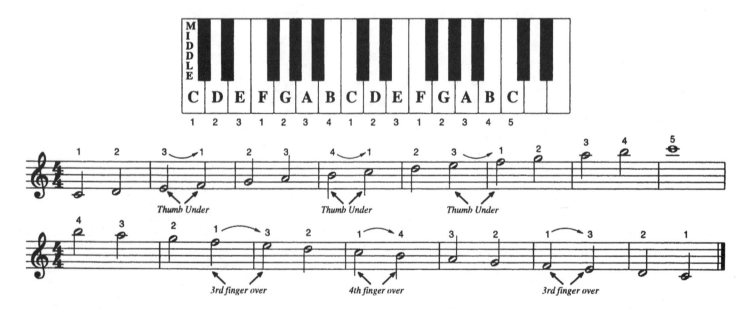

Practice Hints:

Practice the C major scale with a metronome at a slow tempo. Play very evenly – without hitting one note harder than another. Gradually increase the tempo over time. It is more important to play it clean and steady than fast at this stage.

Example 28: G Major Scale

Let's explore some new scales. Play all the white keys on the keyboard from G to G and see if it sounds like the C major scale.

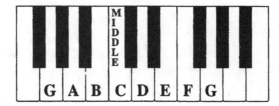

Does it sound the same as the C major scale? Does it sound like the 7th scale degree (F) is a little bit off? Play it again but this time try raising the 7th step (F) up a half step to the black key next to it (F#).

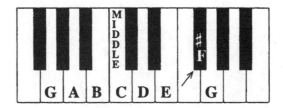

Example 29: Whole Steps – Half Steps

That's it! That scale sounds like the C major scale, just beginning on G. What makes the difference? The scale steps between the 7th and 8th notes of the scale didn't move by 2 notes (a whole step) they moved by 1 note (a half step).

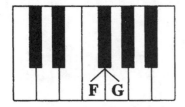

F to G = whole step (W)

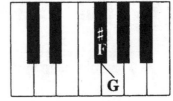

F# to G = half step (h)

Play a 2 octave G major scale using the same fingerings learned on page 25 for the C major scale.

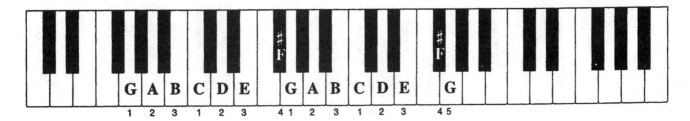

Example 30: F Major Scale

Play the white keys from F to F and see if it sounds like the C or G major scales.

One note doesn't sound right (4th scale degree – B). Try another note there; lower the B a half step to the nearest black key – B♭.

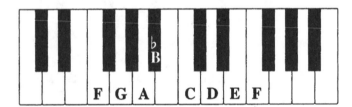

That sounds correct. In addition to the half step between scale degrees 7 and 8, we have discovered there is also a half step between the 3rd and 4th scale degrees in the major scale, as shown below.

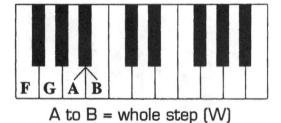

A to B = whole step (W)

A to B♭ = half step (h)

The F major scale uses a different fingering than the C and G major scales. Play a 2 octave major scale using the fingerings indicated below.

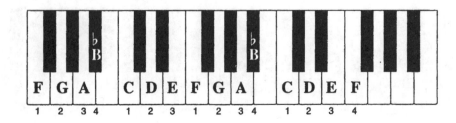

Example 31: Major Scale Formula

All major scales are built with the following formula.

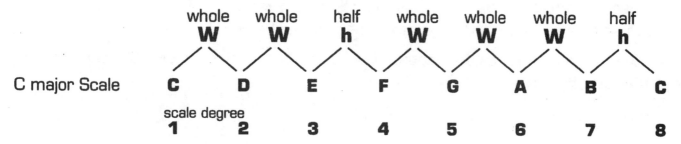

As we discussed in the previous major scales, there are half steps between the 3rd and 4th scale steps and the 7th and 8th scale steps. With this information, you can build a major scale starting on any note. Here is one on B♭.

B♭ major Scale

The B♭ major scale uses a different fingering than any other major scale. Play a 2 octave B♭ major scale using the fingerings indicated below.

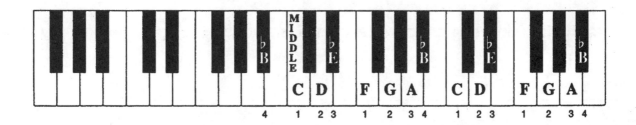

CHALLENGE! Build a major scale from any key on the keyboard. There is a major scale chart on page 106 for your reference.

Example 32: Learning Melodies by Ear

A melody is the part of a song that is sung. There are two ways to learn to play melodies:

    1. Reading music – usually requires the help of a teacher.
    2. Playing by ear – converting what you hear to the keyboard.

Both methods and techniques are important skills to develop. This section will focus on playing melodies by ear.

Right Hand Melody

Listen along with the video to this familiar melody in the key of C and try to find the notes on your own keyboard. Use E as your starting note.

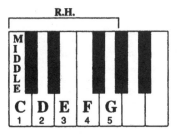

Left Hand Accompaniment

Play the following left hand chord accompaniment with the right hand melody.

Put the right hand melody together with the left hand accompaniment.

CHALLENGE! Use the technique listed above to play other familiar melodies by ear.

Example 33: Improvisation

We've learned a little about scales and about playing melodies by ear; now let's explore improvisation.

Improvisation means making up your own melodies from the notes of the scale. All you need is a little technique and a lot of imagination.

Let's go back to our familiar key of C. With only white keys to deal with it's hard to make a mistake.

First we'll need a chord progression so that we will have a background for our improvised melody. We can pick any chords from the key. Let's start with two; C major and A minor.

C major

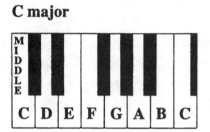

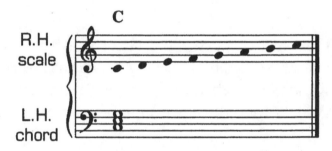

A minor

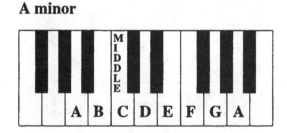

Example 34: Listening

This track is an example of improvising over the C major and A minor chords. The keyboard player plays a C chord with the left hand and the notes of the C scale in the right hand in any order he chooses. The chord changes to A minor in the left hand and the keyboard player continues to improvise with the right hand using the notes in the C major scale.

As you listen to the recording, notice the keyboard player plays basically the same notes over both chords, yet the notes sound very different when played over each chord. Hearing the relationship of a scale to a chord is the essence of improvising.

Example 35: It's Your Turn

Now try some improvising of your own. The recording will repeat the C major and A minor chords as indicated below, allowing you to stretch-out and have some fun. Experimenting with improvisation is how we all learn.

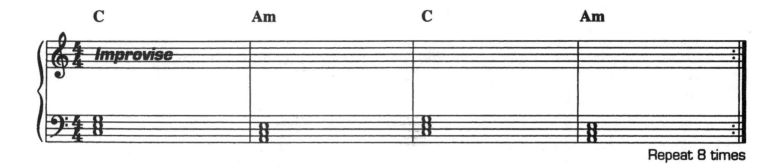

Repeat 8 times

While experimenting you probably noticed that some notes sounded stronger than others. These notes are probably the ones that belonged to the same chord that was being played that moment. When the right hand plays the same notes that are being played in the chords in the left hand, they match.

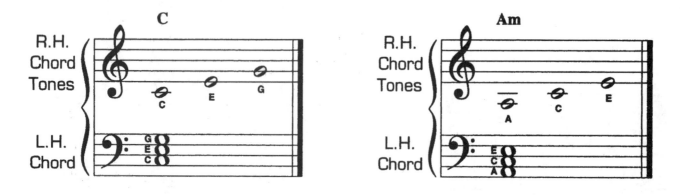

Play Example 35 again. This time try to connect those chord tones with other notes from the scale (passing tones). This will allow you to build your melody with enough other choices to make it sound interesting.

MINOR SCALES

So far we have focused primarily on major scales. Another important sound is minor. Believe it or not, you've already played a minor scale. When you played all the white keys over the Am chord on pages 30 and 31, you played an A minor scale.

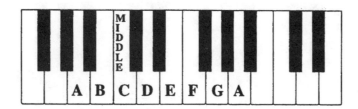

Example 36: Minor Scale Formula

The minor scale, like the major scale, is made up of whole and half steps. In minor, there is a half step between the 2nd and 3rd steps and the 5th and 6th steps of the scale. The rest are whole steps.

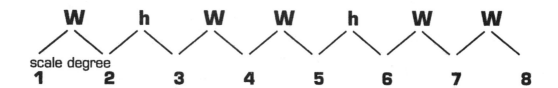

Example 37: A Minor Scale

Looking at the A minor scale, you'll see that the half steps are between B & C and E & F.

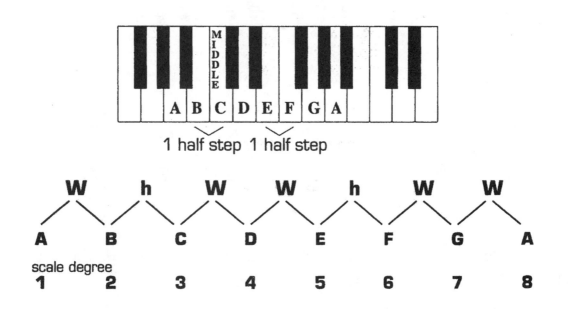

Example 38: E Minor Scale

Let's try this formula starting on E.

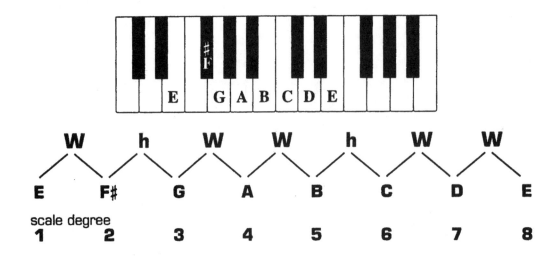

Example 39: D Minor Scale

Now let's try the same scale starting on D.

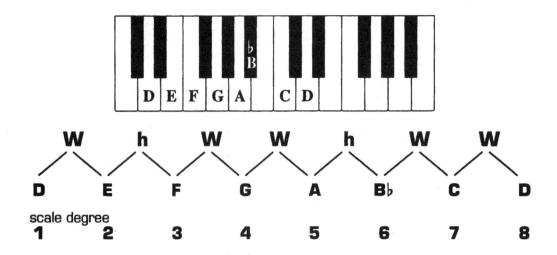

CHALLENGE! Build a minor scale starting on any key on the keyboard. There is a minor scale chart on page 107 for your reference.

Example 40: Relative Minor

If you continue building minor scales on different keys, you'll notice that they all resemble the major scales starting a step and a half higher in pitch. Major and minor scales that are related in this way are actually called "relative" scales.

For example: The A minor and C major scales use the same notes. They are relative scales.

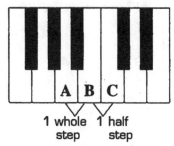

A to C = 1 whole step and 1 half step

A minor scale: A B C D E F G A

C major scale: C D E F G A B C

Example 41

If you look at the E minor and G major scales, the same thing applies. They both have F#s in them.

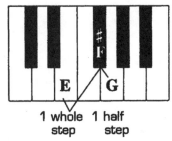

E to G = 1 whole step and 1 half step

E minor scale: E F# G A B C D E

G major scale: G A B C D E F# G

Example 42

Finally, let's look at D minor and F major. They both have B♭s in them.

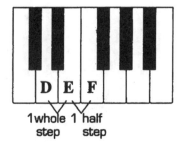

1 whole 1 half
step step

D to F = 1 whole step and 1 half step

D minor scale: D E F G A B♭ C D

F major scale: F G A B♭ C D E F

Review

• What is the whole and half step formula for major scales?

• Build a major scale starting on D.

• What is the whole and half step formula for minor scales?

• Build a minor scale starting on B.

Example 43: The Blues Scale

So far we've covered major and minor scales, but there is one more scale sound that all musicians play – the Blues scale. The sound of a Blues scale is a little different from major and minor scales. The following is a Blues scale in the key of C.

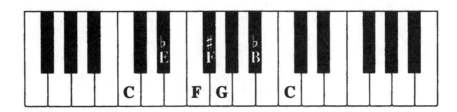

The notes of a Blues scale improvised in any octave on the keyboard will sound great over a Blues chord progression in the key of C. This scale is a lot of fun because you really can't hit a bad note. Let's try the fingering for this scale.

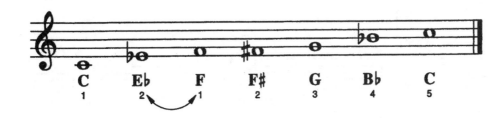

Example 44

Play the Blues chords as indicated below. The song will repeat three times. Listen to the piano player on the recording improvise using the notes of the C Blues scale while you play the chords.

C Blues

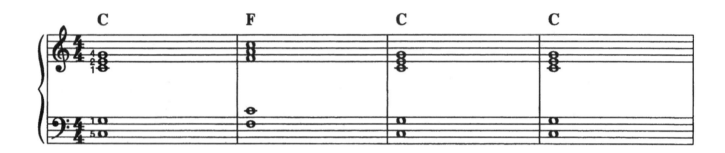

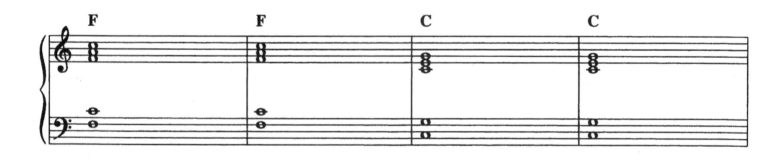

Repeat 3 times

*Last time end on a C chord.

Example 45

Now it's your turn! Improvise over the C Blues utilizing the notes in the C Blues scale as shown below. In the beginning, try to play a chord tone on the first beat of each measure. A suggested chord tone is included in parentheses in each measure to serve as a guide.

C Blues Scale

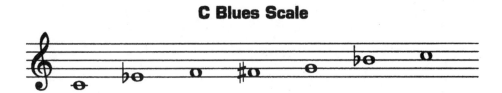

C Blues

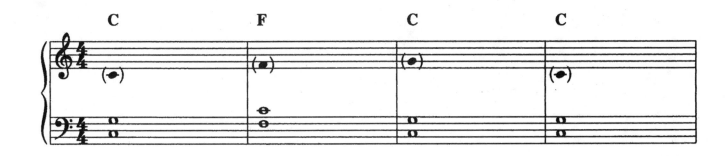

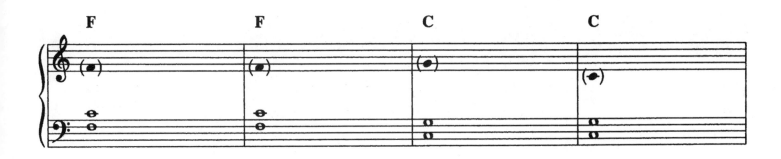

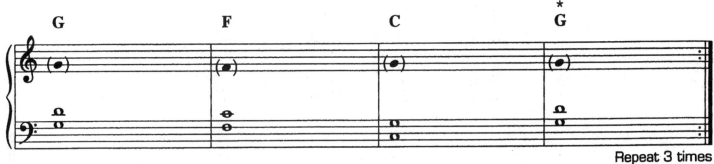

Repeat 3 times
*Last time end on a C chord

BLUES KEYBOARD

Review Chords

CHORDS are made up of 3 or more notes played simultaneously. They are an important part of playing most styles of music including the Blues and Rock and Roll. We are going to focus on the major chord which is made up of the 1st, 3rd, and 5th notes (or scale tones) of the major scale. Let's try one in the key of C.

KEY OF C

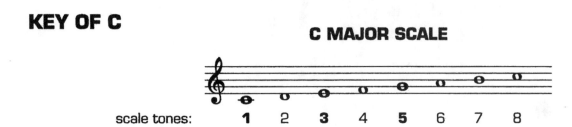

C Chord

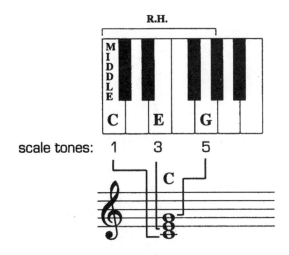

Chords can be written on a music staff using music notation or they can be indicated in the form of a letter called a chord symbol which is located just above the staff. The examples in this book use both.

Play the C chords in the exercise below using your right hand thumb on the C, index finger on the E and the 3rd finger on the G; as indicated by the fingering numbers next to the first C chord.

Now let's try building major chords in the keys of F and G.

KEY OF F

F MAJOR SCALE

F Chord

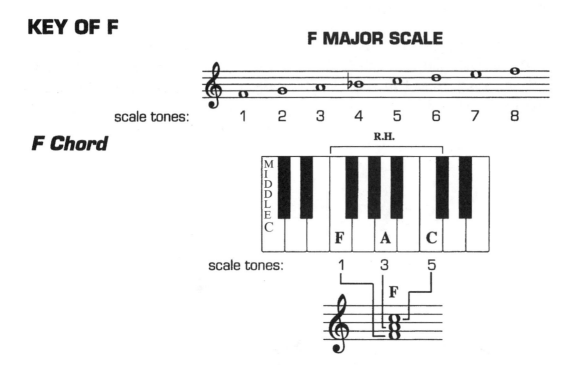

Try the 4 bar example below using the F and C chords.

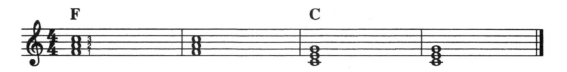

KEY OF G

G MAJOR SCALE

G Chord

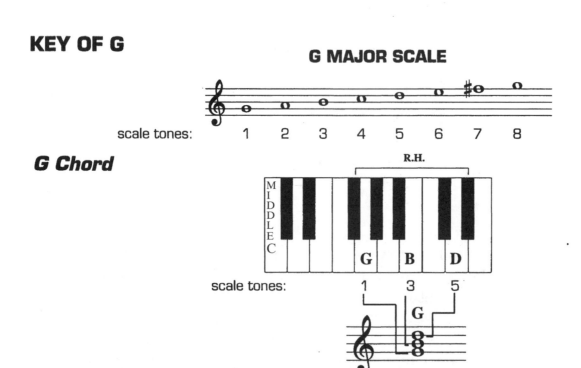

Try the 4 bar example below using the G, F and C chords.

Example 46: 12-Bar Blues Progression

The basic musical form in blues is called the 12-BAR BLUES PROGRESSION. The 12-bar blues progression is made up of three chords in a particular order. The chords are taken from the major scale of the key. For example, in the key of C, when we play the I chord or the C chord it is built on the 1st scale step (or tonic) in the key of C. The IV chord or the F chord is built on the 4th scale step and the V chord or the G chord is built on the 5th scale step in the key of C.

KEY OF C

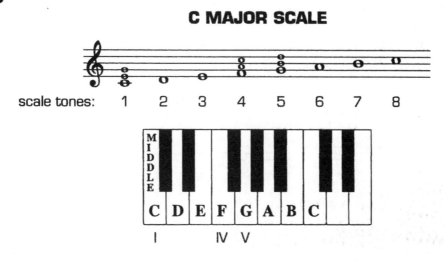

Try playing the four bar example below using the I, IV and V chords in the key of C. Add the root of each chord in the bass with your left hand as indicated below.

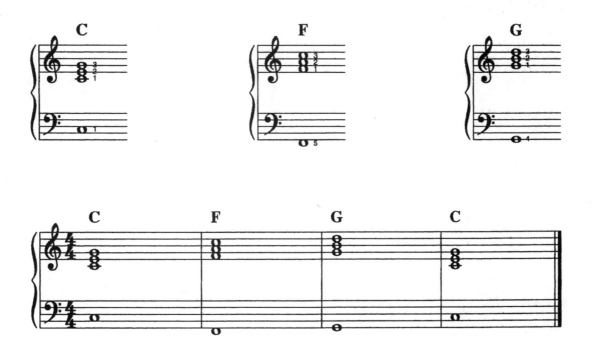

Throughout this section we are going to focus on the key of C, but it is important to try and apply what you learn to the other keys as well.

PLAYIN' THE BLUES

Now let's play the 12-bar blues. The video will go through the progression slowly with verbal cues, then will play through the progression two times up-to-tempo. Hold each chord for four counts.

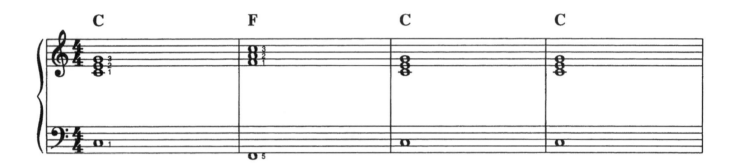

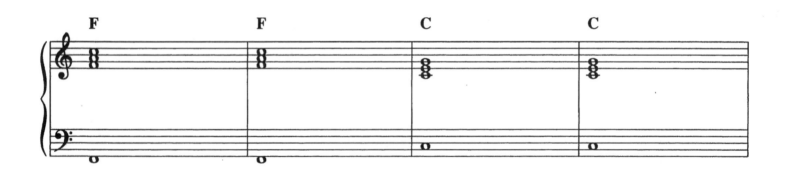

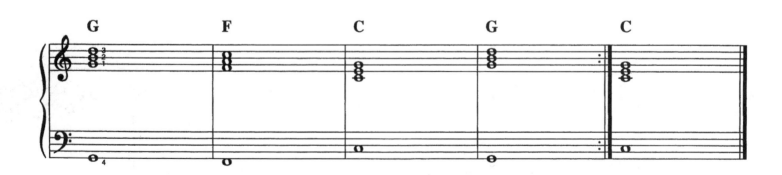

Example 47: Straight Eighth Notes

Earlier we played a 12-bar blues progression based on a straight eighth note feel.

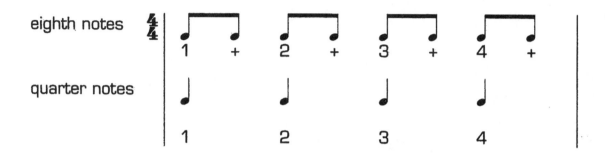

Example 48: Eighth Note Triplets - The Shuffle

The Shuffle is a different rhythmic approach based on an eighth note triplet. There are 3 eighth notes tc every quarter note in an eighth note triplet.

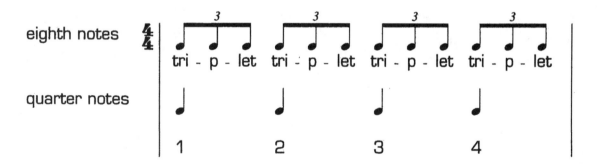

Example 49: Shuffle Feel

The shuffle feel emphasizes the 1st and 3rd triplet and leaves out the middle triplet.

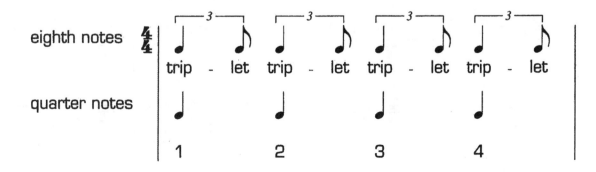

Example 50: Left Hand - Shuffle Pattern on C

Listen to this short example of a shuffle blues feel. The left hand pattern played at the beginning of this track is an important pattern for the shuffle blues. Let's try it. Play C and G with the left hand. Use finger number 5 for the C and 2 for G and play them at the same time leaving your thumb open to play the A. The pattern switches back and forth from C and G playing together to C and A. This is a very nice little pattern for the blues.

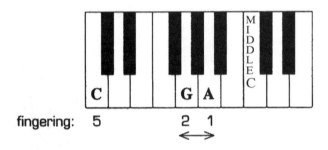

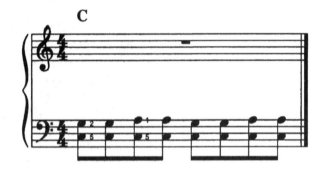

Listen to the example of the left hand shuffle pattern below and then try to play along.

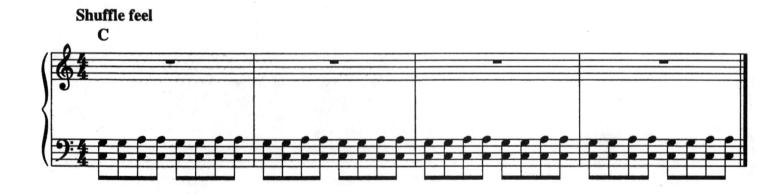

Example 51: Left Hand - Shuffle Pattern on F

Now let's try the left hand shuffle pattern on F. Use finger 5 on the F, finger 2 on C and your thumb on D. Switch back and forth between the two positions as you did with the same pattern on C.

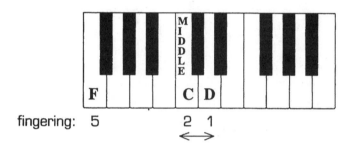

Listen to the example of the left hand shuffle pattern below and then try to play along.

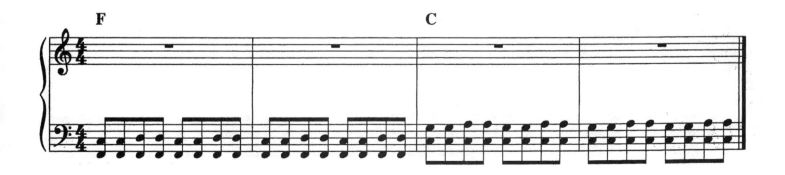

Example 52: Left Hand - Shuffle Pattern on G

Now let's try the left hand shuffle pattern on G. Use finger 5 on the G, finger 2 on D and your thumb on E. Switch back and forth between the two positions as you did for the left hand shuffle patterns on C and F.

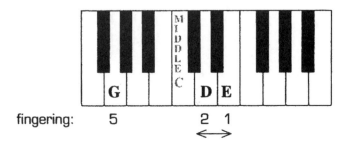

Listen to the example of the left hand shuffle pattern below and then try to play along.

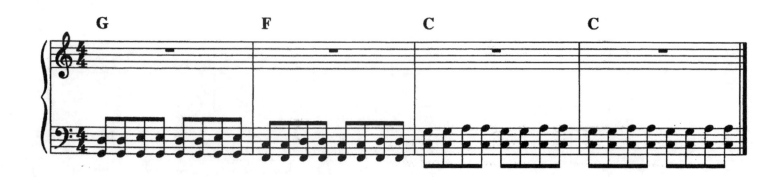

12-BAR BLUES

This example will take you through the 12-bar blues progression with verbal cues. Practice the left hand blues pattern you just learned.

Next try playing along with the 12-bar blues using your left hand pattern. If you need more help, keep practicing with the verbal cues in the previous play-along track.

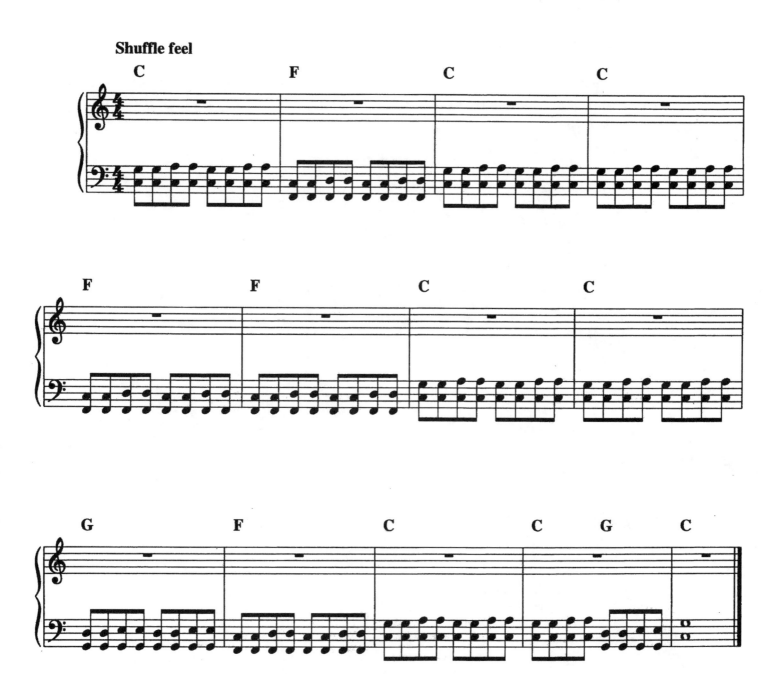

Now that you've learned this shuffle pattern with your left hand, let's add some chords with the right hand.

Example 53: Right Hand - Dominant 7th Chords

Right Hand Shuffle Pattern on C

We are going to use the C, F and G chords learned on pages 40 and 41 for our shuffle blues pattern. To make these chords sound "bluesy," we are going to add an extra note, the flat or dominant 7th. The addition of this note will give our chords an authentic funky-blues sound.

C7 Chord (I7) – Right Hand

As we learned on page 40, a major chord is made up of the 1st, 3rd, and 5th scale tones of the major scale. The dominant 7th chord adds the 7th tone of the major scale but lowers it a half-step.

C MAJOR SCALE

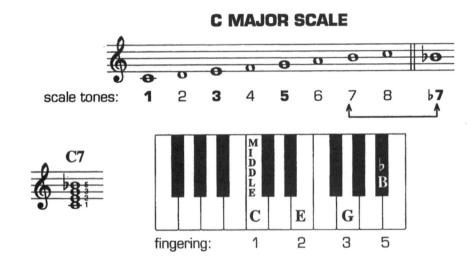

F7 Chord (IV7) – Right Hand

Now let's build an F7 chord.

F MAJOR SCALE

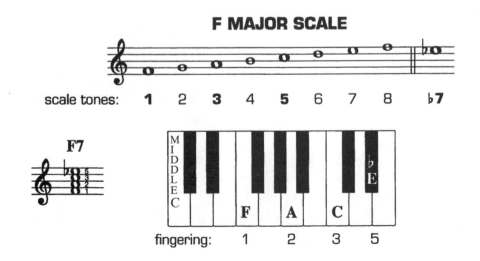

G7 Chord (V⁷) – Right Hand

Now let's build a G7 chord.

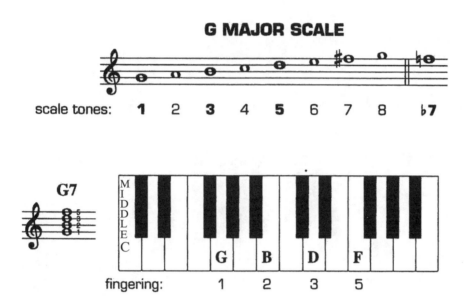

G MAJOR SCALE

scale tones: **1**   2   **3**   4   **5**   6   7   8   ♭**7**

fingering: 1   2   3   5

Try playing the 4 bar example below using the I7, IV7 and V7 chords in the key of C. Let your thumb be your guide when jumping from one position to the next with the right hand.

Example 54: Inversions

Now we are going to play these dominant 7th (or ♭7th) chords in a new position called an INVERSION. The notes of an inverted chord are placed differently than our basic root position chords. Inversions help keyboard players and guitarists make smooth transitions between chord changes, without having to move their hands all over the place. Let's try some inversions.

C7 (I⁷)

This first chord will remain in the root position with the C on the bottom.

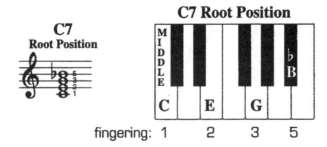

F7 (IV⁷)

The F7 chord is written out below in root position. We are going to create an F7 inversion by moving the top 2 notes down an octave.

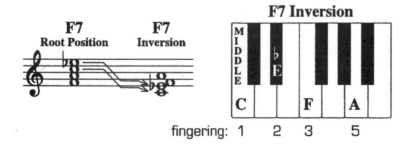

Try moving back and forth between C7 in root position and the F7 inversion you just learned. Notice this transition only requires the movement of 3 notes.

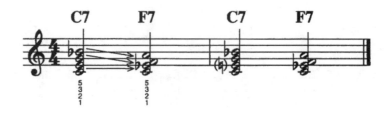

G7 (V⁷)

The G7 chord is written out below in root position. We are going to create a G7 inversion by moving the top 2 notes down one octave.

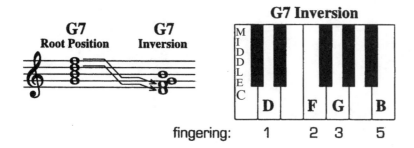

Let's try moving from C7 to F7 to G7 using the inverted positions you just learned.

Example 55: Shuffle Pattern Hands Together

Now that we know how to play these parts with the hands separately, let's try them with the hands working together. You may find it a little difficult at first to hit the right notes while looking at one hand or the other. You may find it helpful to stay on one chord for a while and then move to the next chord after you get the hang of it. That's OK. Just make sure that eventually you are playing the entire 12-bar blues pattern. With a little practice you'll be able to do it without looking at your hands at all.

12-BAR BLUES
SHUFFLE PATTERN – HANDS TOGETHER

Follow along with the video through the 12-bar blues form slowly.

Next, the 12-bar blues form up-to-tempo.

Now watch and listen to a live band play the 12-bar blues.

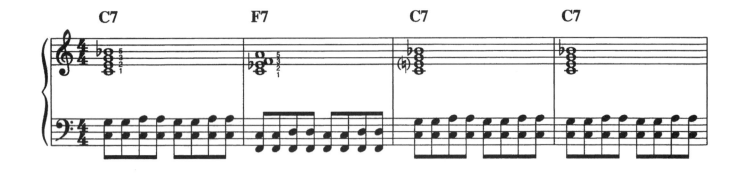

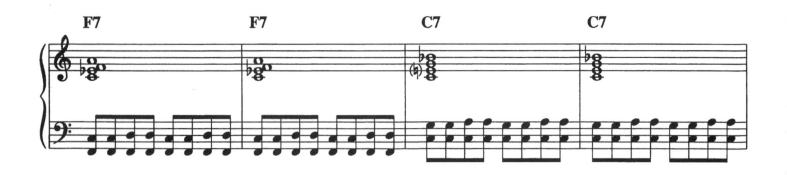

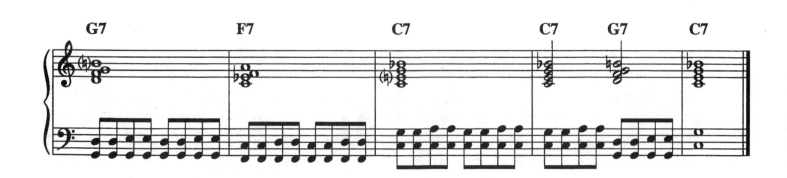

Example 56: Triplet Feel

As we learned on page 44, a song with a triplet feel has an underlying rhythm of 1, 2, 3, for each beat or quarter note pulse. Listen to the example and try to tap or clap 1, 2, 3 for each quarter note pulse. A hand clap sound plays the eighth note triplets on the recording for your reference.

Triplet feel

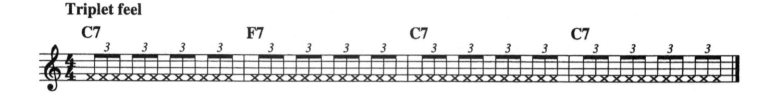

Example 57: Triplet Feel – Left Hand Pattern

Remember Fats Domino? His blues style piano playing helped to popularize those great New Orleans style triplet patterns that we might hear on a tune like Blueberry Hill. We're going to learn one of those patterns using the left hand to outline a melody in the bass, which can really spice things up. This is a very simple pattern with a very interesting sound. Let's try it out.

You might have noticed at the beginning of the previous performance that the keyboard player was sliding off the black keys to give the bass line a more authentic sound. First, we'll learn the notes, then we'll add the black key slide. The bass line is an arpeggiated pattern. An ARPEGGIO is the notes of a chord played one at a time.

C Arpeggio Bass Line – Left Hand

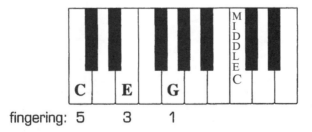

fingering: 5   3   1

F Arpeggio Bass Line – Left Hand

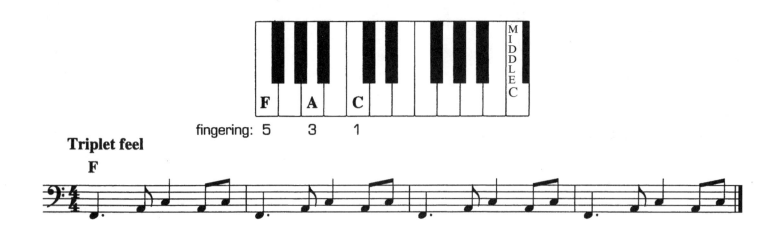

G Arpeggio Bass Line – Left Hand

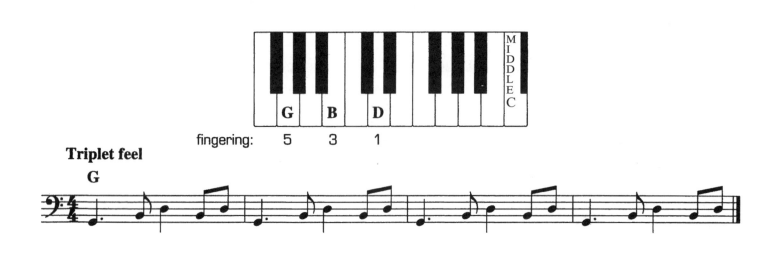

Practice this left hand bass arpeggio pattern using the 12-bar blues progression at a slow tempo, then slowly increase as you get more comfortable with it.

Example 58: Triplet Feel Left Hand Pattern – Adding the Black Key Slide

Example 58 plays through the I, IV and V left hand arpeggios adding the black key slide.

C Chord (I)

For the bass pattern on the C chord, play the E♭ with your 3rd finger of your left hand and slide into the E (which is the note we are targeting anyway).

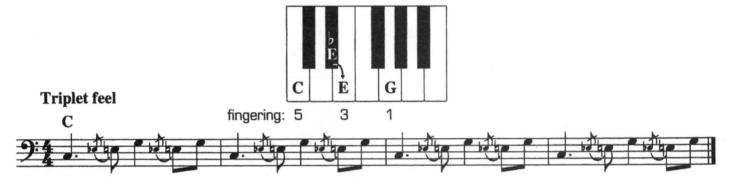

F Chord (IV)

Now move up to the F position and play the A♭ with the middle finger of your left hand and slide into the A.

G Chord (V)

In the G position play the B♭ with the middle finger of your left hand and slide into the B.

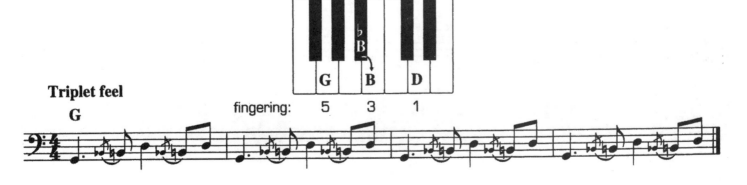

12-BAR BLUES

Now let's try putting the left hand triplet pattern with the black key slide, together with the right hand dominant 7th chords and inversions through the entire 12-bar blues progression.

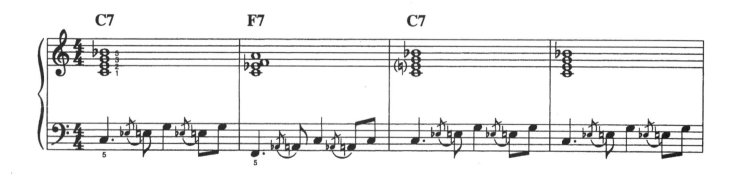

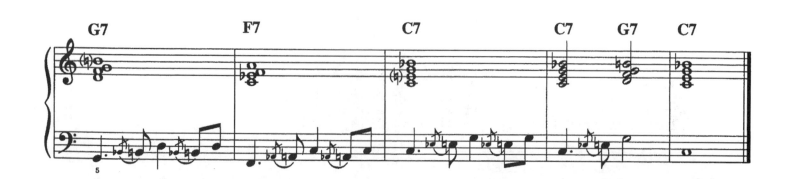

Example 59: Triplet Feel – Right Hand Pattern

In this example, two things have changed since our shuffle blues pattern in Example 50. First, the rhythm is different. Instead of playing a shuffle feel we are playing all three notes in the eighth note triplet.

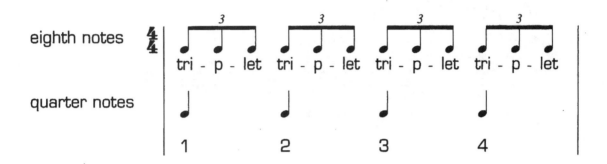

Second, we've changed some of the notes in the chord structure to give them a different feeling. The C chord contains the note A which is the 6th note or scale tone of the C major scale making the chord a C6.

C6 Chord

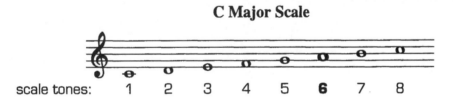

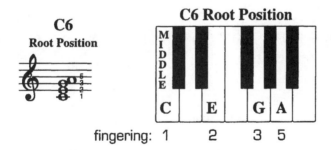

To play the C6 chord in an inversion we will raise the note C up one octave.

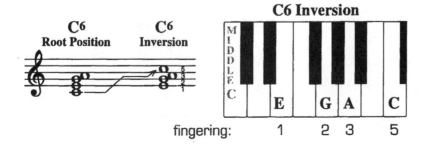

F9 Chord

The F7 chord we are going to use for the triplet pattern contains an extra note added to the dominant 7th chord as well. The extra note is called the 9th. If you count up the F major scale to the 9th scale degree, you will get a G. So, the new note added to our chord voicing is G making our chord an F9 chord. The F9 inversion lowers the E♭ and G notes 1 octave from the root position. When playing an F9 inversion it is not necessary to include the note F.

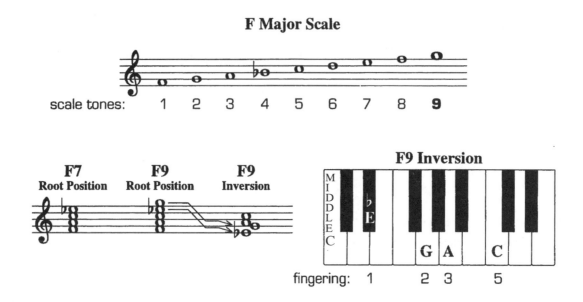

G9 Chord

The G9 chord also contains the 9th scale degree of the G major scale which is the note A. The G9 inversion lowers the F and A notes 1 octave from the root position. When playing the G9 inversion it is not necessary to include the note G.

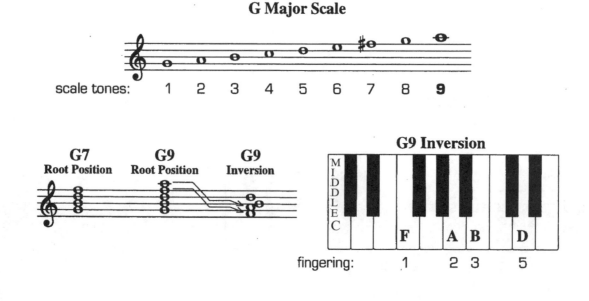

Now play through the 12-bar blues progression below with the video to practice your new right hand chord voicings, paying particular attention to the more difficult parts.

Try playing the right hand triplet chords in the 12-bar blues with the band.

12-BAR BLUES

Practice Hints!

Practice these patterns slowly at first and then increase the speed. If you find your right hand getting tired it may be because you're using the arm muscles instead of the wrist and finger muscles. Be sure to relax, keep good posture, breathe and use the wrist muscles and you'll get it in no time.

62

Example 60: Triplet Feel – Hands Together

Now that we can play each hand separately, let's put them together. The challenging part of putting the two hands together is eliminating mistakes from the pattern. The main thing we need to do in order to avoid mistakes is to work on the transitions within each pattern. In other words, we have to work on each change to make different chord shapes. Keep working on this very slowly until you get it.

Next is an example of a 12-bar blues with a triplet shuffle feel. It plays through the entire form one time.

Now it's your turn. The keyboards have been removed from this track allowing you to be the star. This track plays through the 12-bar blues form two times.

TRIPLET-FEEL BLUES

Example 61: Shuffle Boogie – Right Hand

Now we are going to explore another shuffle pattern called the SHUFFLE BOOGIE. It takes what you already know and adds a little rhythm to the right hand. The left hand pattern is exactly the same as we learned on page 45, so we will concentrate on the rhythm of the right hand.

Try to clap along.

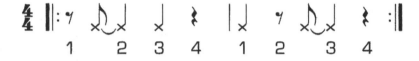

SHUFFLE BOOGIE

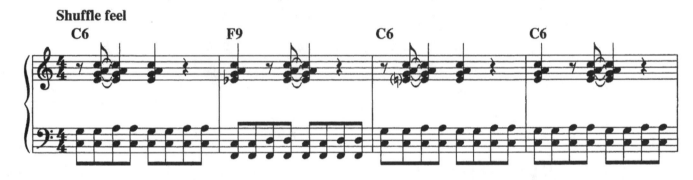

A very important part of the blues progression is the turnaround. A TURNAROUND is the name we give to the last two bars of the blues progression. It is where you finish up a song and get get ready to "turn around" and go back to the top. There are a few very traditional turnaround phrases that all blues players have come to know. Let's explore some of them now.

Example 62: Turnaround #1

Let's separate the right left hand parts of this turnaround and then put it all together.

Turnaround #1 – Left Hand

Turnaround #1 – Right Hand

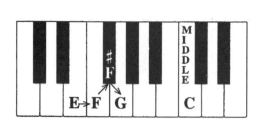

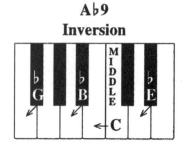

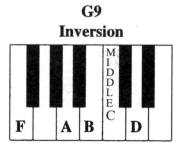

Turnaround #1 – Hands Together

Now let's play a 12-bar shuffle boogie blues with turnaround #1. Go back and play the shuffle boogie on page 62. When you get to the 2 bars before the repeat sign, play turnaround #1 instead of what is written.

Example 63: Turnaround #2

The first turnaround we played is useful and basic, but the one we're going to learn now is THE turn around for the blues. We will call it turnaround #2. You will probably recognize turnaround #2 as soon as you hear it. Let's separate the right and left hand parts of this turnaround and then put it all together.

Turnaround #2 – Left Hand

The left hand pattern is mainly a single note melody with a different ending. The motion of the melody is mostly chromatic. CHROMATIC means that the notes are moving by half steps.

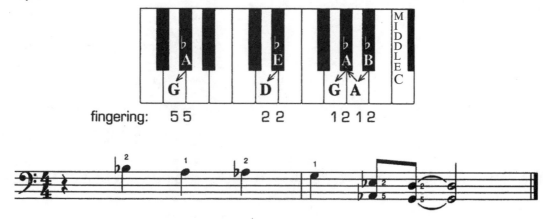

Turnaround #2 – Right Hand

The right hand pattern starts with an inverted C7 chord as shown below.

To start this turnaround the thumb is playing an E, the 2nd finger is playing a G, the 3rd finger is on the Bb and the 5th finger is playing a C. All of the notes move down the keyboard by half steps except for the 5th finger which stays on the C. Continue the downward motion until you reach a root position C chord with fingers 1, 2, and 3.

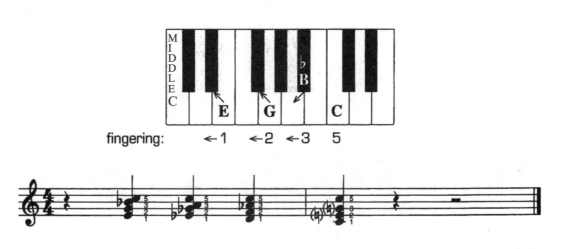

Turnaround #2 doesn't play all of the notes in the right hand position at the same time. instead it rocks back and forth in an eighth note triplet pattern between the two lower and the two higher notes in each chord.

The last 2 chords for turnaround #2 (Ab9 and G9) are notated below. We learned these chords earlier in turnaround #1 on page 63.

Turnaround #2 – Hands Together

Are you ready to put the two hands together? Remember, it's important to not practice mistakes so make sure you have it in each hand separately before trying to put it together. It's also very important to be patient about learning these patterns. You'll find that even after you've practiced for a short period of time, you'll get it. This pattern will be a lot of fun and you'll get a lot of mileage out of it.

Listen to this example of turnaround #2 with the hands together followed by turnaround #2 being played in the context of the last 4 bars of the blues progression. Try to play along.

Every time the 12-bar blues progression ends and the band is going to continue to play the song, there is a turnaround. Each member of the band plays the turnaround in his own way. Whenever you see a blues band, pay attention to the turnarounds they play. This will help you learn more turnaround ideas.

Example 64: Blues Ending #1

You may have noticed that when the band got to the end of the tune, they played a couple of different chords instead of the usual turnaround progression. This is called a BLUES ENDING. Let's take a look at this and learn how to play it.

Blues ending #1 is just like turnaround #2 except for the last two chords. The last two chords are 9th chords (just like the Ab9 and the G9 chords we played earlier in turnaround #2.) The 9th chords used for this blues ending are Db9 and C9.

Blues Ending #1 - Right Hand

Db9 Chord

To play the Db9 chord with your right hand, put your thumb on the Cb (or B), your 2nd finger on Eb, your 3rd finger on F and your 5th finger on Ab.

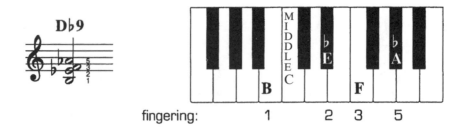

C9 Chord

The notes we play for the C9 chord are Bb with your thumb, D with your 2nd finger, E with your 3rd finger and G with your 5th finger.

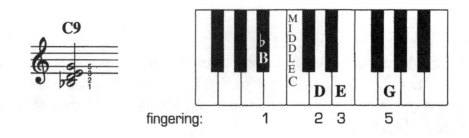

Blues Ending #1 – Left Hand

Now let's try the left hand. Play the left hand pattern you learned for turnaround #2 but change the last two notes to D♭ and C.

 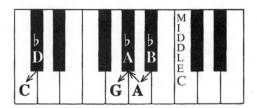

Blues Ending #1 – Hands Together

Now let's try playing the right hand and left hand parts together as notated below. Practice slowly.

Blues soloing is probably the most fun you can have at the keyboard, but it does involve some experience and some basic skills around which to develop your musical ideas. Some favorite blues keyboard players like Professor Longhair, Ray Charles and Charles Brown are responsible for a lot of the ideas we will explore in this book. What all of these players do to make their playing unique is to improvise within the blues. So far, we've concentrated on chords and rhythm. Now we are going to add melody to the mix, and melodies are based on scales. What we are going to look at first is the BLUES SCALE.

Example 65: The Blues Scale In C

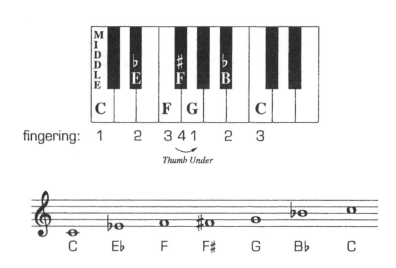

Example 66: Blues Scale In C – Two Octaves

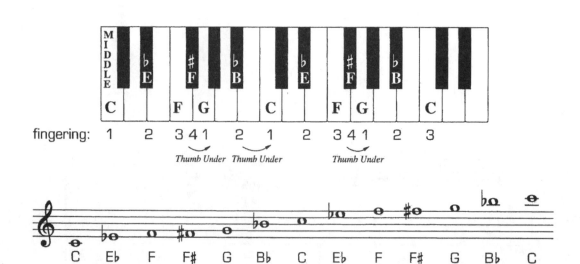

Example 67: C Major Pentatonic Scale

The major pentatonic scale is also very common in blues soloing. This scale has a brighter, happier sound than the blues scale. It has five notes, which is where the name pentatonic comes from.

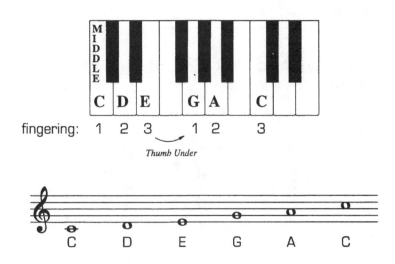

Example 68: C Major Pentatonic Scale – 2 Octaves

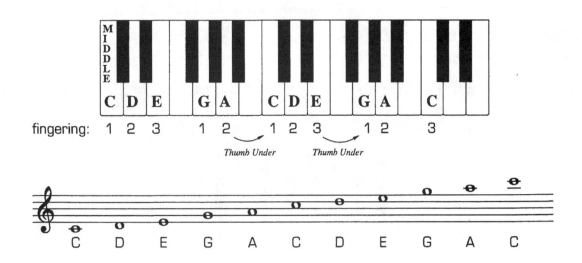

You may notice that the pentatonic scale sounds more like the major scale than the blues scale does. The pentatonic scale will give us some different notes to play and will make the blues scale sound even better when we play it again. Compare the sound of these two scales in the key of C.

Next, listen to the organ solo using the blues and major pentatonic scales. See if you can tell when the soloist uses the blues scale, and when he uses the major pentatonic scale in his solo.

A blues LICK means a phrase or a melody that is played so many times by so many different players in improvisation that it actually becomes part of the musical language. Let's try some licks.

Example 69: Blues Lick #1

This lick is exactly like the blues scale in C going downward. Use the 3rd finger to play the black key slide from F♯ to F♮.

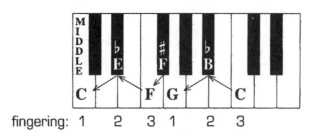

fingering: 1   2   3 1   2   3

Example 70: Blues Lick #2

This lick begins with the E♭ sliding to E with the thumb and then uses the notes from the C6 chord.

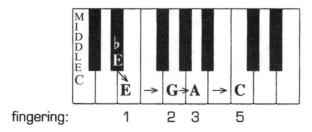

fingering: 1   2 3   5

Starting on beat 2.

Starting on beat 1.

Example 71: Blues Lick #1 and #2 Combined

1. upward

2. downward

Example 72: Blues Lick #3

Blues lick #3 is demonstrated in two versions below. The first one works well when soloing over the V chord and the second one works well when soloing over the IV chord in a 12-bar blues progression.

G7 (V7)

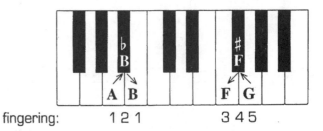

fingering: 1 2 1   3 4 5

F7 (IV7)

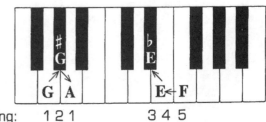

fingering: 1 2 1   3 4 5

OK. Are you ready to jam? Let's take the 12-bar blues pattern and play some of these new licks over it. The keyboard player on the recording will play one of the licks then you can play it back the same way after him. Finally, he will play the chords of the 12-bar blues progression and you can just combine the scales and licks you've learned into a cool solo. Have fun!

12-BAR BLUES – SOLOING

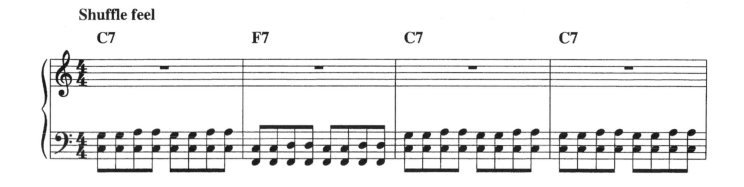

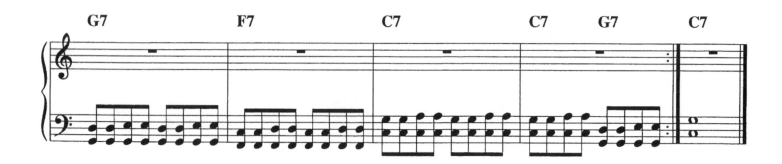

ROCK KEYBOARD

Example 73: The Blues

THE BLUES FORM

It is said that Rock and Roll, Jazz, and even some country music were all derived from the Blues. In fact, the first Rock and Roll ever recorded was called "Blues Part Two" by a group of well-known jazz artists in the mid to late 1950s. In this section, we'll review the basics of the Blues, but apply it to keys more closely related to Rock keyboard playing.

12 BAR BLUES

To review, the Blues is what we call a I, IV, V progression. I, IV, V refers to the positions of the key that we are in. Let's start in the key of G. The root position or the tonic or I note is G, count up to C for the IV and up one more to D for the V.

Key of G

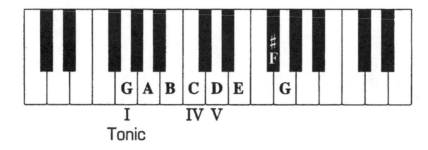

The most common Blues form is the 12 Bar Blues. As noted on page 6, a bar is 4 beats in length. The 12 Bar Blues form is commonly used so that people can play together as a group and jam.

12 Bar Blues form

```
4 | I    | I    | I    | I    |
4 | G    | G    | G    | G    |

  | IV   | IV   | I    | I    |
  | C    | C    | G    | G    |

  | V    | IV   | I    | I    ||
  | D    | C    | G    | G    ||
```

Example 74: Chords

Chords are made up of 3 or more notes played simultaneously. Chords are an important part of playing most styles of music including the Blues and Rock and Roll. We are going to focus on the dominant 7th chord which is made up of the 1st, 3rd, 5th and dominant 7th (or ♭7th) notes of the major scale – as shown below.

Since our 12 Bar Blues is in the key of G, we will start with the G dominant 7th chord (written G7).

G7 CHORD (I)

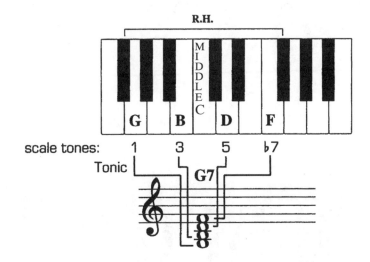

Chords can be written on a music staff using music notation or they can be indicated in the form of a letter called a chord symbol which is located just above the staff. The exercises in this book use both.

Play the G7 chords in the exercise below using your right hand thumb on the G, index finger on the B, 3rd finger on the D and your pinky on the F as shown in the fingering numbers next to the first G7 chord.

C7 CHORD (IV)

Now let's move up to the IV chord in the key of G which is the C7 and play it for 2 bars followed by 2 bars of G7 as indicated below.

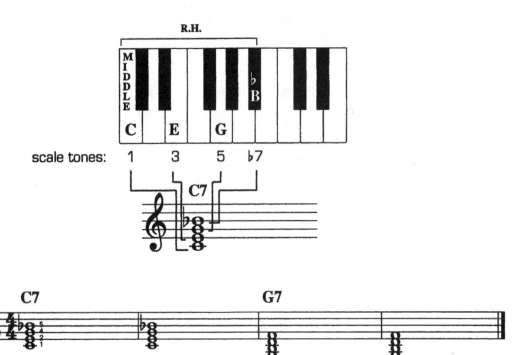

If a chord repeats in the next bar you don't usually repeat its name above the staff.

D7 CHORD (V)

Try the V chord in the key of G (D7). Play the exercise below using the D7, C7 and G7 chords.

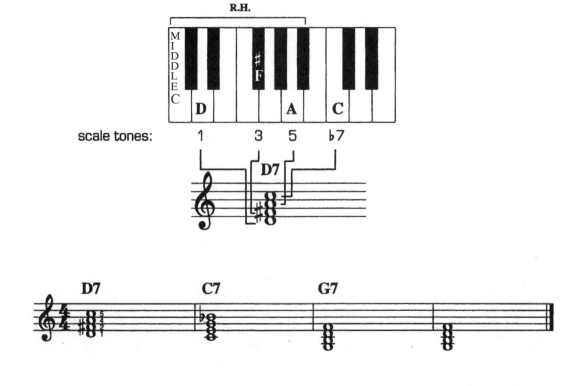

Example 75: 12 Bar Blues in G

Now that you can play the I, IV and V chords in the key of G, try playing through the entire 12 Bar Blues form using your right hand.

12 BAR BLUES

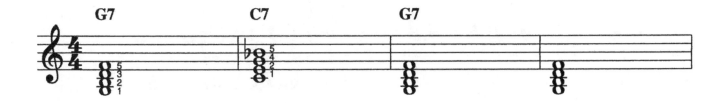

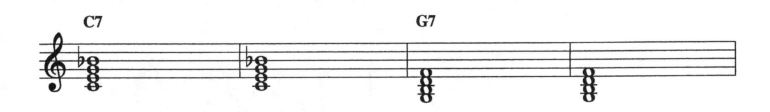

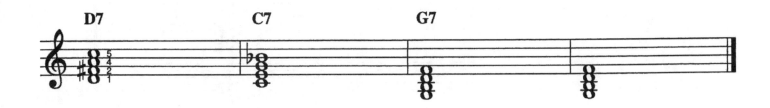

CHORD VOICINGS

A voicing is the placement of chord notes (or chord tones) on a keyboard. There are many different voicing combinations available for chords. Let's experiment with two different voicings for right now.

Example 76: Basic Voicing Position

A basic voicing position is similar to the one learned on pages 76 and 77. To complete that basic voicing, the root can be added by the left hand in the bass clef as indicated below.

Example 77: Full Sounding Voicing Position

This voicing can contain the root on the bottom and the top of the chord.

G7 CHORD (I)

The left hand pinky is on the root (G), the index finger is on the 5th (D). The right hand thumb is on the ♭7th (F), the index finger is on the 3rd (B), the 3rd finger is on the 5th (D), and the pinky is on the root (G). Play the voicing then try the 4 bar example below.

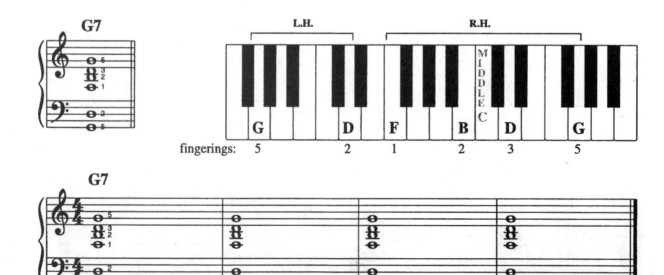

C7 CHORD (IV)

The left hand pinky is on the root (C), the index finger is on the 5th (G). The right hand is playing the ♭7th with the thumb (B♭), the index finger is on the 3rd (E), the 3rd finger is on the 5th (G), and the pinky on the root (C). Play the voicing then try the 4 bar example below.

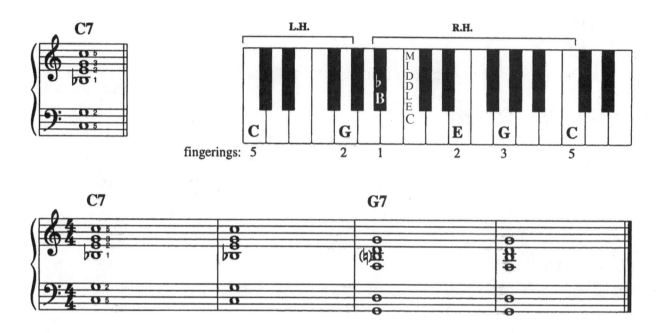

D7 CHORD (V)

The left hand pinky is on the root (D), the index finger is on the 5th (A). The right hand thumb is on the ♭7th (C), the index finger is on the 3rd (F#), the 3rd finger is on the 5th (A), and the pinky is on the root (D). Play the voicing then try the 4 bar example below.

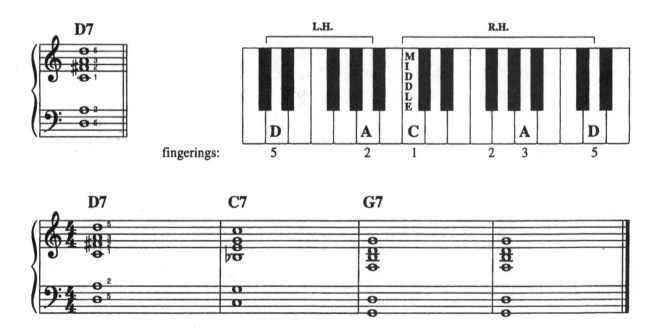

82

Example 78: *Selecting a Sound*

Now that we have voicings to play we need to select the right sound. If you're playing an electric keyboard or a synthesizer, you've got plenty of sounds to choose from. Some of the most common choices for Rock are:

• PIANO
• ORGAN
• ELECTRIC PIANO
• HONKY TONK PIANO

For this first Blues, let's stick with the electric piano sound.

Example 79: *Parts*

Now we have the sound, but what do we actually play? We know the form of the tune, we know the chords and how to play them, but now we need to come up with a part.

Example 80:
Basic Rock Keyboard Part on the I chord (G7)

1. The left hand is playing the pinky on the root (G) and the index finger on the 5th (D). The right hand is playing the ♭7th with the thumb (F), the 3rd with the middle finger (B), [There is a *grace note from the minor 3rd (which is a black key – B♭) to the third (B).] and the 5th with the pinky (D).

 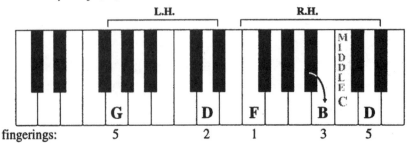

2. The first position now moves up the keyboard by one note for each finger. The left hand pinky remains on the G and the left hand thumb moves up to E. The right hand thumb moves up to G, the middle finger plays C and the pinky is on E.

 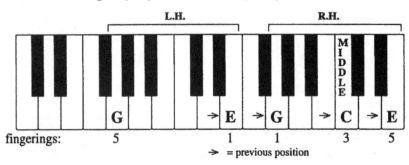

*Grace Note: A note of very short duration, which takes some of the value of the preceding note.

3. Now we need to move up one more position as shown below. The left hand pinky remains on the G and the left hand thumb goes up to F which is the dominant 7th. The right hand thumb moves up to A, the middle finger plays D and the pinky is on the F.

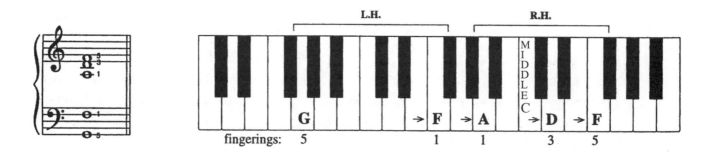

Below is a graphic representation of the new basic Rock keyboard part you just learned on the G7 or I chord. Try to put it all together by moving up and down between the three positions.

● = 1st position of part.
■ = 2nd position of part.
▲ = 3rd position of part.

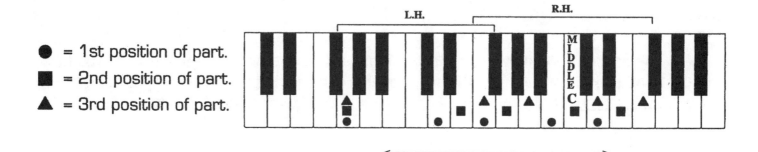

Below is an example of the new G7 Rock part written out musically on a grand staff.

This was an example of a basic rock riff using the I chord in the key of G. Next we will learn to play that same part on the IV and V chords which are the chords we need to play the 12 bar blues.

84

Example 81:
Basic Rock Keyboard Part on the IV chord (C7)

To learn that part on the IV chord, we are going to put our hands on the same notes but up an even fourth to a C7 voicing.

1. The left hand plays the root with the pinky (C) and the 5th with the index finger (G). The right hand plays the dominant 7th with the thumb (B♭), the 3rd with the index finger (E), [There is a grace note from the minor 3rd (which is a black key E♭) to the third (E).] and the 5th with the middle finger (G).

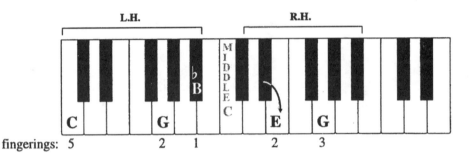

2. The first position now moves up the keyboard by one note for each finger. The left hand pinky remains on the C and the left hand thumb plays A. The right hand thumb moves up to C, the index finger plays F and the fourth finger is on A.

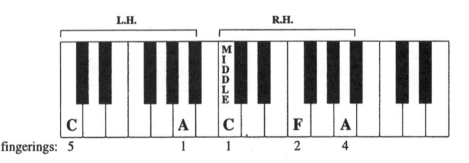

3. We need to move up one more position as shown below. The left hand pinky remains on the C and the left hand thumb goes up to B♭ which is the dominant 7th. The right hand thumb moves up to D, the middle finger plays G and the pinky is on the B♭.

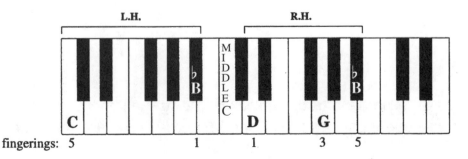

Below is an example of our new rock part on the IV or C7 chord written out musically on a grand staff.

Now try moving from 2 bars of G7 to 2 bars of C7.

Example 82:
Basic Rock Keyboard Part on the V chord (D7)

1. The left hand plays the root with the pinky (D) and the 5th with the index finer (A). The right hand plays the dominant 7th with the thumb (C), the 3rd with the middle finger (F#), and the 5th with the pinky (A).

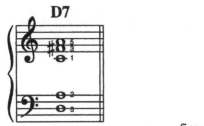
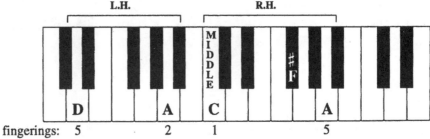

2. The first position now moves up the keyboard by one note for each finger. The left hand pinky remains on the D and the left hand thumb plays B. The right hand thumb moves up to D, the middle finger plays G and the pinky is on B.

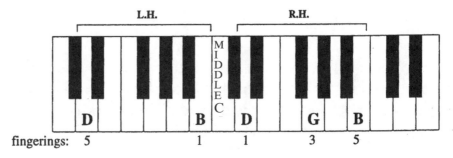

3. We need to move up one more position as shown below. The left hand pinky remains on the D and the left hand thumb goes up to C which is the dominant 7th. The right hand thumb moves up to E, the middle finger plays A, [You can play a grace note here from the A♭ with the 2nd finger to the A with the 3rd finger.] and the pinky is on C.

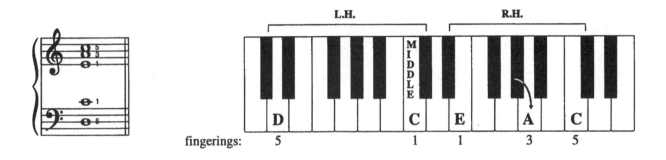

fingerings:

Below is an example of our new rock part on the V or D7 chord written out musically on a grand staff.

Now try moving from 1 bar of D7 to 1 bar of C7 followed by 2 bars of G7 as shown below.

Practice playing the I, IV and V chord parts in the key of G. Try not to play these parts too rigid or precise but remember to keep it loose and have a good feel. Creating your own parts requires experimentation, experience and taking a few risks. The only way to come up with something cool is to try out new ideas.

Example 83: 12 Bar Blues with Parts

Now let's put the parts we just learned on the I, IV and V chords together in a 12 Bar Blues.

Listen to the band play the 12 Bar Blues below. Pay attention to the piano player as he plays the parts you just learned. The song will repeat 3 times.

Now it's your turn! The band will play the 12 Bar Blues again but this time without the piano part, allowing you to be the star. The song will repeat 3 times. Play the parts you learned as written below, and try to make up some of your own. Have fun!

12 BAR BLUES

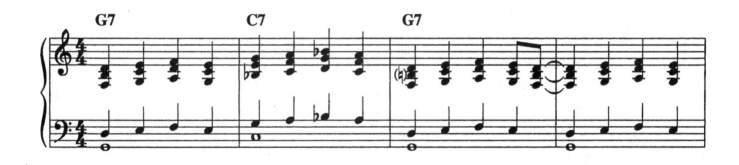

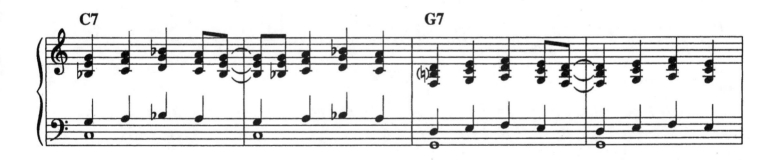

Repeat 3 times
*Last time end on G7

Example 84: Part Variations

Now let's see how these new parts sound with a few variations.

After you become comfortable with the basic parts and voicings throughout the book, it's fun to explore with variations. A few popular variation techniques include:

1. Adding the root:

One variation includes adding the root with the right hand pinky above the rest of the voicing. Below is an example on the G7 chord.

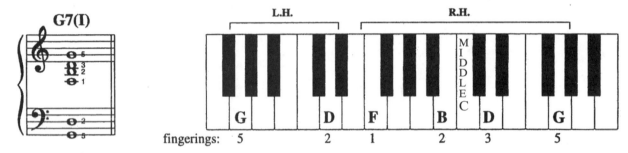

2. I to IV chord transition:

Instead of moving the hands up to the IV chord position, let's try just moving one of the notes in the I chord position and adding the 3rd to form the IV chord.

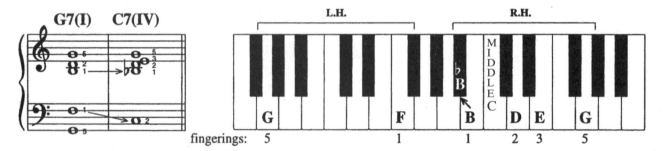

3. Eliminating notes

This part (or riff) drops off some of the extra notes we used before in the voicing and only uses the root (G) and the 3rd of the chord as a starting point. The three notes in the middle move up and down as in the parts we learned before.

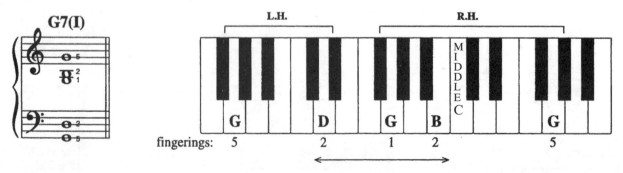

Challenge!

Try to learn the 3 variations listed above in all 12 keys. This will greatly enhance your playing.

SOLOING — IMPROVISING

Improvisation means making up your own melodies from the notes of the scale. All you need is a little technique and a lot of imagination. There is a lot you can do with soloing (improvising, jamming, riffing) as a keyboard player. There are endless varieties and possibilities. Let's get started with some basic techniques for soloing and improvising.

There are many different kinds of scales in music. As we discovered on page 8, if you play all the white keys from C to C on the keyboard, you are playing the C major scale. We are now going to explore a different scale which we will use for soloing called the blues scale.

Example 85: The Blues Scale

The notes of the blues scale improvised in any octave on the keyboard sound great when played over a blues chord progression. This scale is a lot of fun because you really can't hit a bad note. Let's try one in the key of G.

Blues Scale in G

notes	G	Bb	C	Db (C#)	D	F	G
scale tones	1	b3	4	b5	5	b7	1

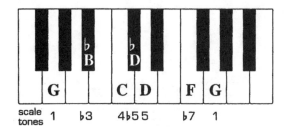

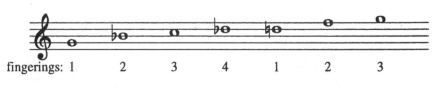

fingerings: 1 2 3 4 1 2 3

Blues Scale in G with added 3rd

In addition to the notes in the blues scale, sometimes it's fun to add the 3rd scale tone to give it a little more flavor and variety.

notes	G	Bb	B	C	Db (C#)	D	F	G
scale tones	1	b3	3	4	b5	5	b7	1

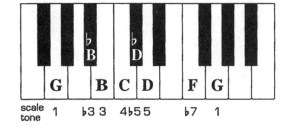

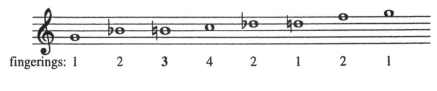

fingerings: 1 2 3 4 2 1 2 1

Challenge!

Try making up patterns using the notes of the blues scale. Improvising provides you with an opportunity to express yourself. Listen to recordings of your favorite performers, hear different ideas and try to figure out what they are playing. Try to learn the blues scale in all 12 keys. A blues scale chart has been provided for your reference on page 108.

Example 86: 12 Bar Blues

Play the blues chord voicings as indicated below. The song will repeat 3 times. Listen to the piano player on the recording improvise using the notes of the G blues scale while you play the chords using whole notes.

Now it's your turn! This time play only the left hand chord voicings and use your right hand to improvise with the notes of the G blues scale.

G Blues Scale

G   Bb   C   Db   D   F   G

12 BAR BLUES

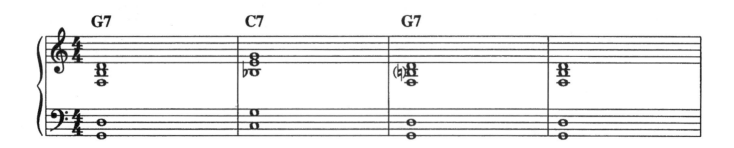

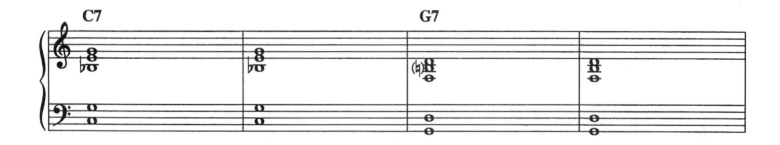

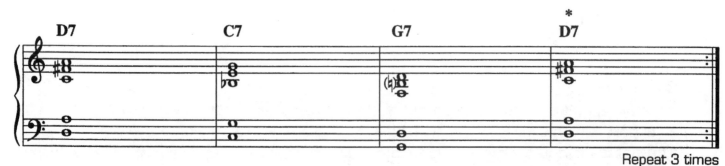

Repeat 3 times
*Last time end on a G7 chord

Example 87: Comping

Comping is a rhythmic accompaniment that is played to back up and support a soloist. Try the shuffle-style comping examples below. Listen to the recording and then try to play along.

Shuffle feel

Shuffle feel

Listen to the Shuffle Blues. Notice that the piano player uses the same notes of the blues scale when soloing, but approaches the rhythms with a shuffle feel rather than with straight eighth notes.

Next is an example of a 12 Bar Blues with a shuffle feel. The song will repeat 3 times. Listen to the piano player on the recording improvise using the notes on the G blues scale with a shuffle feel while you play the chords utilizing the comping patterns written out below.

Now it's your turn! This time play only the left hand voicings and use your right hand to improvise using the notes of the G blues scale with a shuffle feel.

SHUFFLE BLUES IN G

Repeat 3 times
*Last time end on G7

It is important to come up with your own rhythms while comping. Listen to the examples on the video and make up your own rhythmic comping patterns using the play-along track. Experiment with comping and have fun!

Example 88: Mixolydian Mode

Another scale often used in soloing/improvisation over Rock and Roll is the mixolydian mode. The mixolydian mode is just like the major scale except it has a ♭7th. The dominant 7th chord that you've been playing uses notes from this scale/mode. In the key of G, the mixolydian mode uses all of the white keys from G to G. This scale, or mode, gives you more choices than the blues scale for improvisation and lends itself to a different sound.

Key of G

G major scale:	G	A	B	C	D	E	**F♯**	G
scale tones:	1	2	3	4	5	6	**7**	8

G mixolydian mode:	G	A	B	C	D	E	**F**	G
scale tones:	1	2	3	4	5	6	**♭7**	8

G Mixolydian Mode

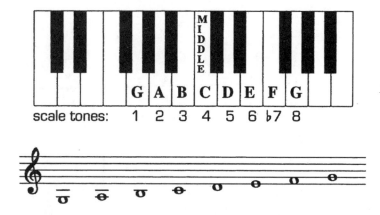

Listen to the piano player improvise over a G7 chord using the G mixolydian scale.

Now it's your turn! Try improvising over a G7 chord using a G mixolydian scale. The piano has been removed from the mix giving you a chance to play a solo.

G7

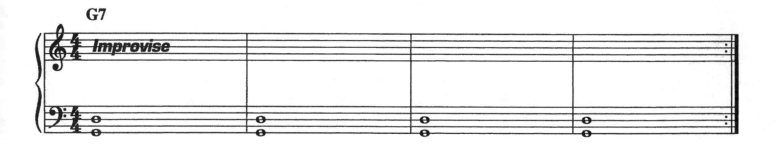

Key of C

C major scale:	C	D	E	F	G	A	**B**	C
scale tones:	1	2	3	4	5	6	**7**	8

C mixolydian mode:	C	D	E	F	G	A	**B♭**	G
scale tones:	1	2	3	4	5	6	**♭7**	8

C Mixolydian Mode

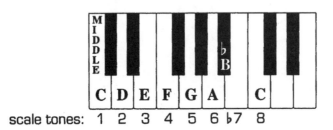

scale tones: 1 2 3 4 5 6 ♭7 8

Key of D

D major scale:	D	E	F#	G	A	B	**C#**	D
scale tones:	1	2	3	4	5	6	**7**	8

D mixolydian mode:	D	E	F#	G	A	B	**C**	D
scale tones:	1	2	3	4	5	6	**♭7**	8

D Mixolydian Mode

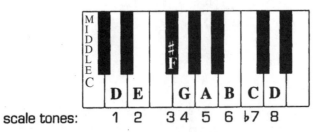

scale tones: 1 2 3 4 5 6 ♭7 8

Example 89: Dorian Mode – Minor 7th Scale

The dorian mode, also known as the minor 7th scale, is just like the major scale except the 3rd and 7th scale tones are flat.

Key of C

C major scale:	C	D	**E**	F	G	A	**B**	C
scale tones:	1	2	**3**	4	5	6	**7**	8
C dorian mode:	C	D	**E♭**	F	G	A	**B♭**	G
scale tones:	1	2	♭**3**	4	5	6	♭**7**	8

C Dorian Mode

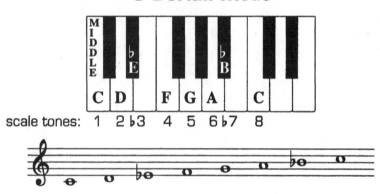

Key of G – A Dorian Mode

You can also think of a dorian mode as being related to any major scale because the dorian mode is really a major scale starting on the 2nd note. So playing eight notes in the key of G starting on A will make an A dorian mode.

G major scale:	G	A	B	C	D	E	F#	G	
scale tones:	1	2	3	4	5	6	7	8	2
A dorian mode:		A	B	C	D	E	F#	G	A

A Dorian Mode

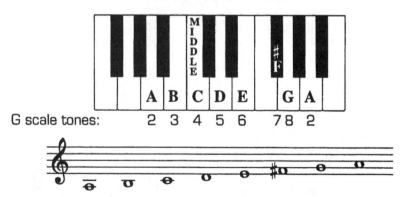

Challenge!

Try to learn the dorian mode in all 12 keys. A dorian mode chart has been provided on page 111 for your reference.

Example 90: Minor 7th Chords

Minor 7th chords (m7) are made from the 1st, 3rd, 5th and 7th notes of the dorian mode, or minor 7th scale. Actually, you can take any note from the scale and put it into your chord voicing (2nd, 4th). We will explore adding more scale tones to chords later, for now we will stick to the basic minor 7th chord tones. Let's build an A minor 7th chord using the 1st, 3rd, 5th and 7th notes from the A dorian mode.

A DORIAN MODE

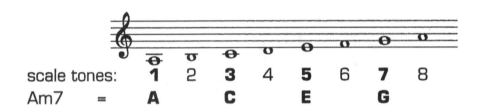

Am7 – Basic Voicing Position

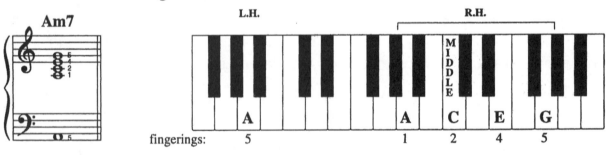

Am7 – Full Sounding Voicing Position

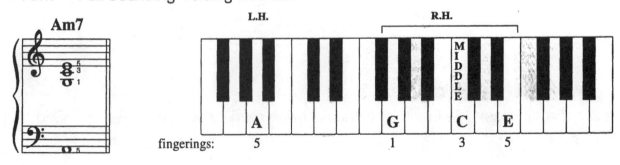

Example 91: Major Chords (add 9)

The Major chord with an added 9th is really the same as a major chord with one additional note – the 9th (also called the 2nd). The additional note enhances the sound of a basic triad or chord, like the ones you learned beginning on page 76.

To better understand the concept of 9ths, let's take a look at a major scale in the key of C.

Key of C

C major scale:	C	D	E	F	G	A	B	C
scale tones:	1	2	3	4	5	6	7	8

If we keep going up the scale and begin writing out a second octave in the key of C, the 9th scale degree is D. (It is also the 2nd.) That is why a major chord with an added 9th is sometimes called a major chord add 2.

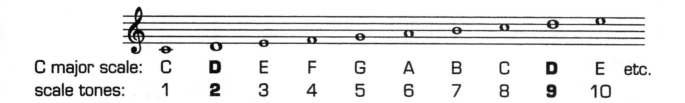

C major scale:	C	D	E	F	G	A	B	C	D	E	etc.
scale tones:	1	2	3	4	5	6	7	8	9	10	

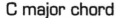

C major chord

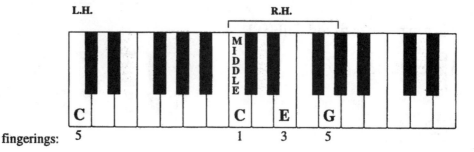

fingerings:

C major chord add 9

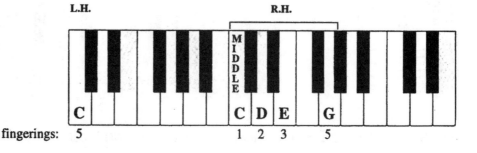

fingerings:

Key of D

D major chord

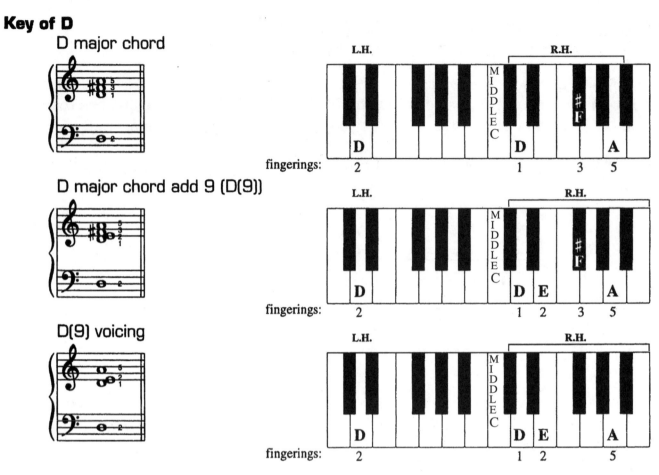

D major chord add 9 (D(9))

D(9) voicing

Key of E

Let's try 9th chords in the key of E

E major chord

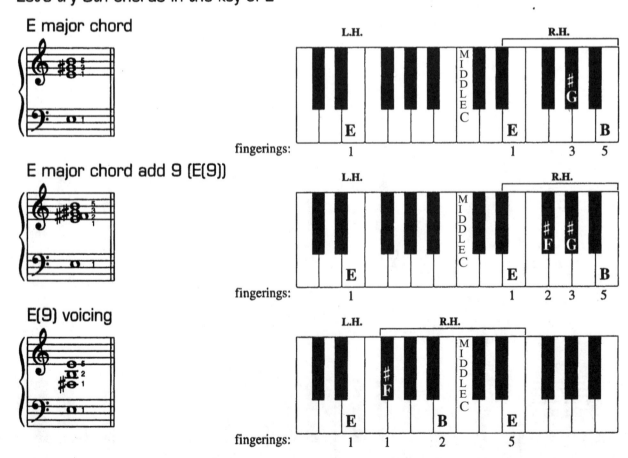

E major chord add 9 (E(9))

E(9) voicing

We will use the E9 and the D9 chord voicings later in SWAMP BOOGIE [page 100].

Example 92: Review — Major Scale, Dorian Mode and Minor 7th Chords

To prepare for our next song, let's review the various scales, modes and chords learned so far in the key of F#.

Key of F#

F# major scale:	F#	G#	**A#**	B	C#	D#	**E#**	F#
scale tones:	1	2	**3**	4	5	6	**7**	8

F# dorian mode:	F#	G#	**A**	B	C#	D#	**E**	F#
scale tones:	1	2	**♭3**	4	5	6	**♭7**	8

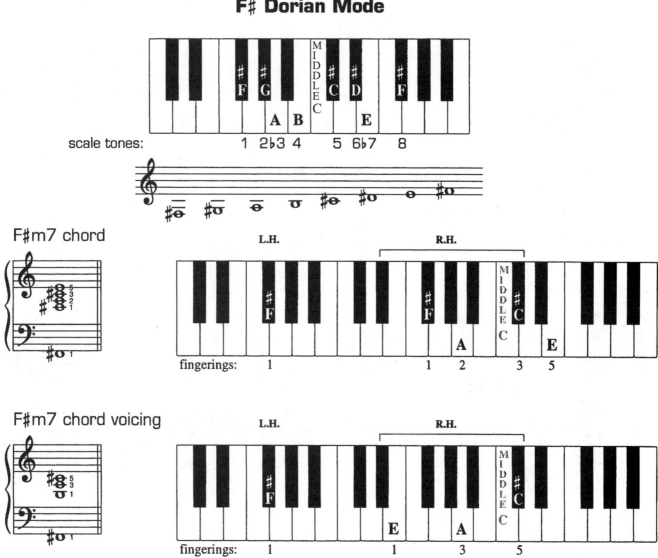

F# Dorian Mode

F#m7 chord

F#m7 chord voicing

We will use the F#m7 chord voicing later in the next song entitled SWAMP BOOGIE [page 100].

Challenge!

Try to learn the minor 7th chords in all 12 keys. Refer to the Dorian Mode chart on page 111. The minor 7th chords are made up of the 1st, 3rd, 5th and 7th notes from the scales in that mode.

Example 93: SWAMP BOOGIE

This song is based on a 12 Bar Blues, but the form is actually 24 bars. As stated before, understanding the form of a song is very important so you know where you are at all times. This song is in the key of A, but we are starting out on the IV chord which is a D7.

You can use the same dominant 7th Blues parts we learned earlier for the D7 and A7 chords. The F♯m7, E9, and D9 chords will use the same voicings we learned in Examples 91 and 92. These chords should be sustained (or held out for the whole measure). They provide the climactic point of the song.

Sample voicings for each chord in SWAMP BOOGIE are shown below. Experiment with these voicings and try to create your own.

SWAMP BOOGIE SAMPLE VOICINGS

D7

D(9)
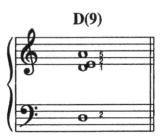

A7
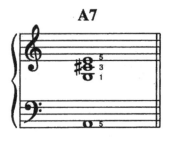

E(9)
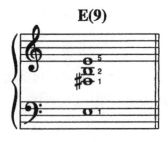

F♯m7

Listen to the band play SWAMP BOOGIE.

Listen to the author describe the form, chords and voicings used in SWAMP BOOGIE.

Now it's your turn! The keyboards have been removed from this recording of SWAMP BOOGIE, allowing you to be the star. Experiment with different voicings and parts. Have fun!

SWAMP BOOGIE

Example 94: Major 7th Chords

Major 7th chords are made up of the root, 3rd, 5th and major 7th notes of the major scale. (We call it a major 7th because it contains a chord tone from the 7th position of the major scale, not a lowered 7th as in the dominant 7th chords we've been playing.)

Key of C

C major scale

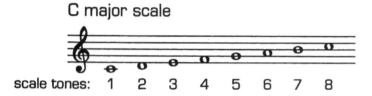

scale tones: 1   2   3   4   5   6   7   8

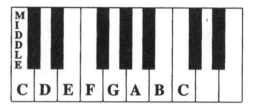

Cmaj7 chord

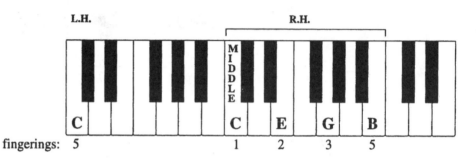

Key of F

F major scale

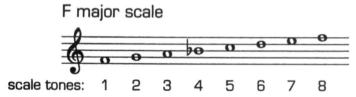

scale tones: 1   2   3   4   5   6   7   8

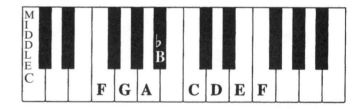

Fmaj7 chord

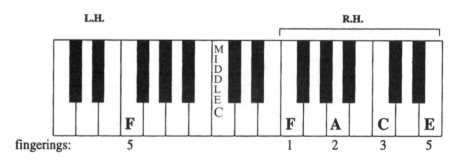

Practice playing the Cmaj7 and Fmaj7 chords as written in the 4 bar example below.

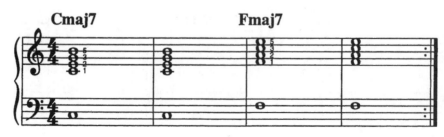

Example 95: Suspended Chords

A suspended chord contains no 3rd in its structure. Instead, it contains the 4th scale tone. A suspended chord can be labeled with more than one name. In the example below, the notes on the keyboard form an A minor 7th chord with a D in the bass. That same combination of notes can also be called a D suspended chord because it contains all the notes for a D chord, except for the 3rd (F#).

Key of D

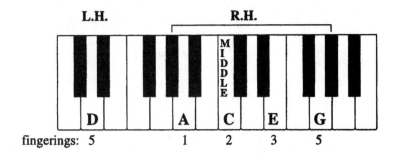

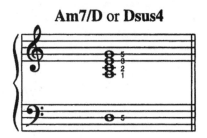

Am7/D or **Dsus4**

Suspended Voicings

One example of a suspended chord voicing is:

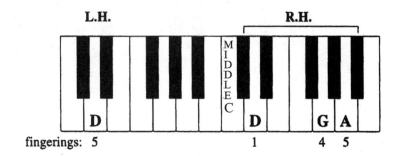

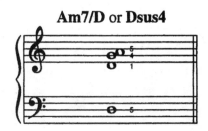

Am7/D or **Dsus4**

Another example of a suspended chord voicing is:

Key of D

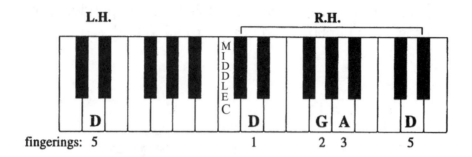

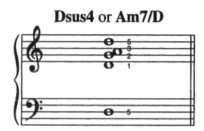

Dsus4 or Am7/D

Typically, the 4th of the suspended chord will resolve to the 3rd forming a major chord as shown below. Our next song entitled Song Example #1 will not resolve its suspended chords to major. This will help to add harmonic interest in the song.

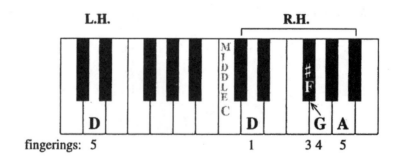

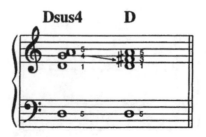

Dsus4   D

Example 96: Song Example #1 — Minor Blues

Listen to the band play Example #1 – Minor Blues. This 20 bar song is an example of a minor blues using minor, major 7th, suspended and major 9 chords.

Listen to the author describe the form, chords and voicings used in Song Example #1 – Minor Blues.

Now it's your turn! The keyboards have been removed from this recording of Song Example #1 – Minor Blues allowing you to be the star. Sample voicings are provided below to get you started. Experiment with different voicings and parts. The A blues scale is also shown below and can be used for improvising over this song.

SAMPLE VOICINGS

Am7   Am7/D (Dsus)   Fmaj7   G9

A BLUES SCALE

Song Example #1 — Minor Blues

$\frac{4}{4}$	Am7	Am7	Am7	Am7
	Am7	Am7	Am7	Am7
	Am7/D	Am7/D	Am7/D	Am7/D
	Am7	Am7	Am7	Am7
	Fmaj7	G9	Am7	Am7 :||

Example 97: Creating Your Own Parts

It is important to create your own parts. The best way to decide what your part should be is to listen to the other members of the band. Play something that will complement and enhance what is being played. Some important points to remember when playing with other members of the band are:

1. DRUMS: Listen to the drummer. Always play in time with the drummer. The drummer is the timekeeper or the metronome of the band. He is the boss of the rhythm. Listen to him for the pulse and the groove of the song. Pay close attention to the Hi-Hat because that is where he is usually going to play the most consistent rhythm, and the Snare Drum which is usually going to play some backbeats.

2. GUITAR: Complement the guitar player. Work around what he is playing. For example, if he is playing a rhythmic part, you might want to play parts that sustain or ring-out called "pads."

If the guitar player is playing sustained-type parts, you might find some staccato rhythmic patterns.

Sometimes the keyboards can support or reinforce the guitar part by doubling (playing the same thing) or playing a simpler part that contains the same phrases and rhythmic emphasis.

It is also important to be "in tune" harmonically with the guitar player by listening to and checking out his voicings and patterns. You may be asked to leave out the 3rd of a chord in a particular voicing.

Sometimes you'll be asked to omit the 5th from a chord voicing.

3. BASS: Watch out for the bass player's area. (The lower register of the keyboard.) Try to keep left hand keyboard parts simple when playing with a bass player. Do not let lower notes sustain or ring out too much. Try to use the left hand as an extension of the right hand, adding more notes and a fuller range to the right hand voicing or part.

4. OVERALL: Listen to the other members of the band. When someone else is soloing, be supportive and back them up. Leave spaces and don't play as loud. When it is your turn to play lead, turn up the volume and don't be afraid to step out there.

Learn to play in other keys. We've worked in G, but learn all 12.

Try variations on all the things we've done. Try to do it your own way. Buy records, CDs and videos — find out what the musicians are playing.

If you are serious about playing, there is no substitute for a real teacher. You can study fingerings, scales, technique, reading, etc. There is no limit as to how far you can progress if you really want to make music. Practice a little bit every day and don't be afraid to try and express yourself.

Example 98: Closing Song

MAJOR SCALES

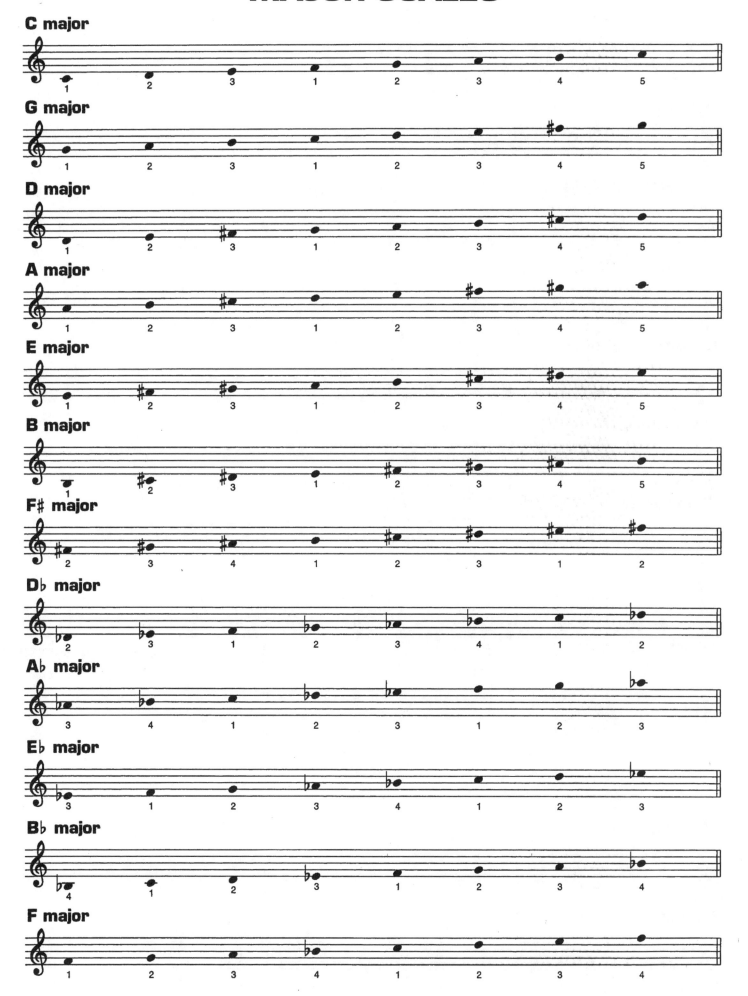

MINOR SCALES

BLUES SCALES

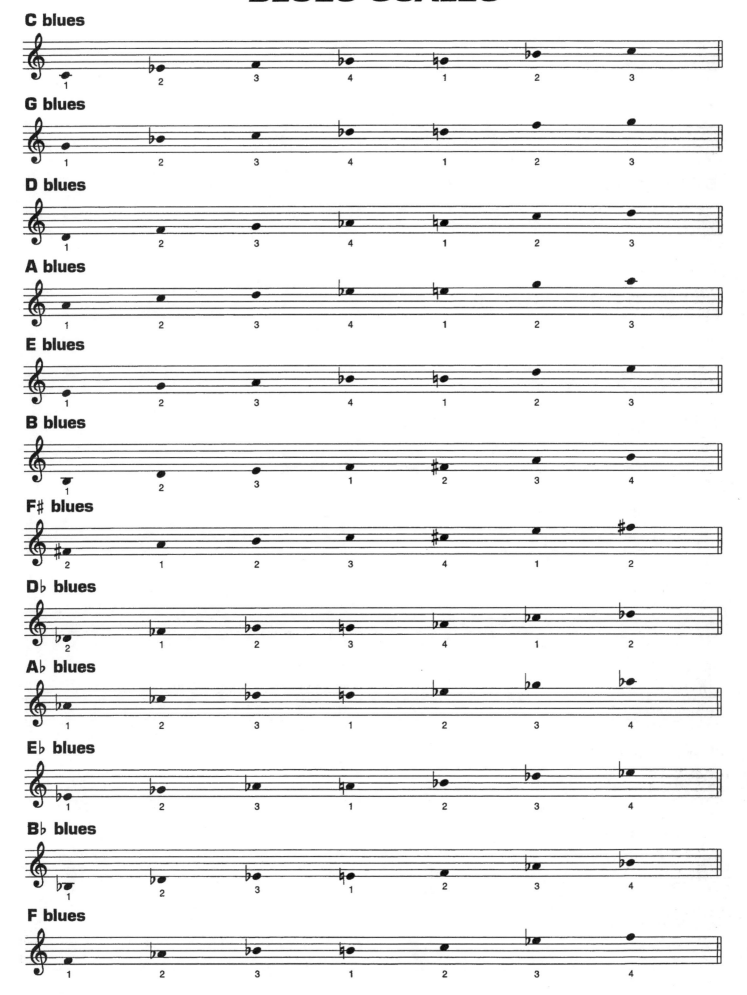

MAJOR PENTATONIC SCALES

MIXOLYDIAN MODE

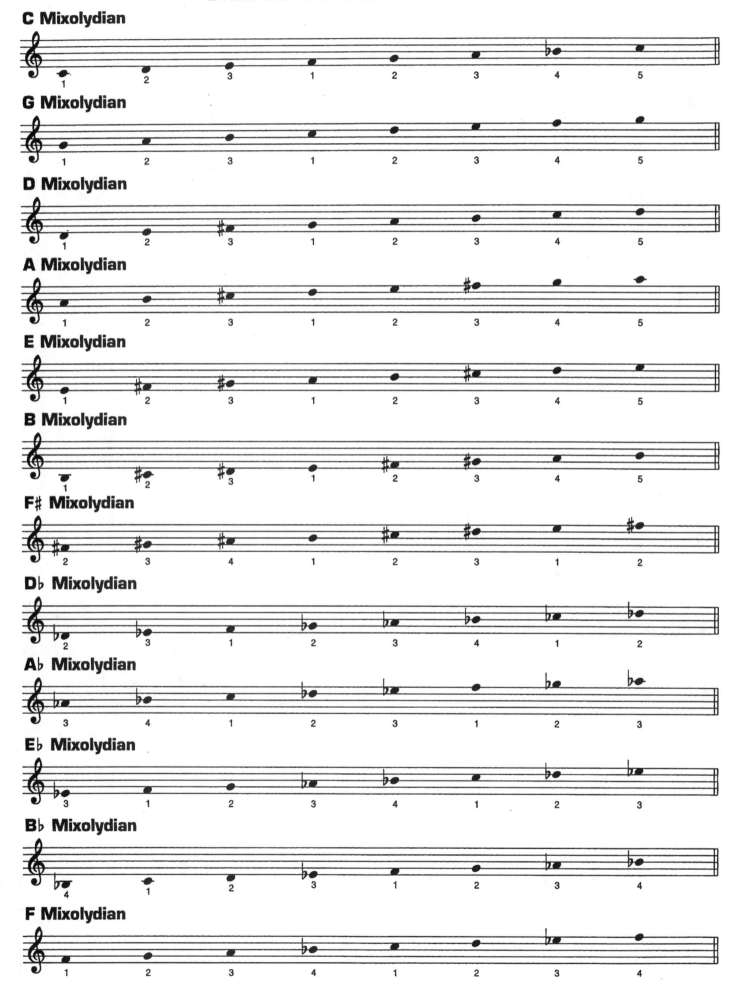

DORIAN MODE

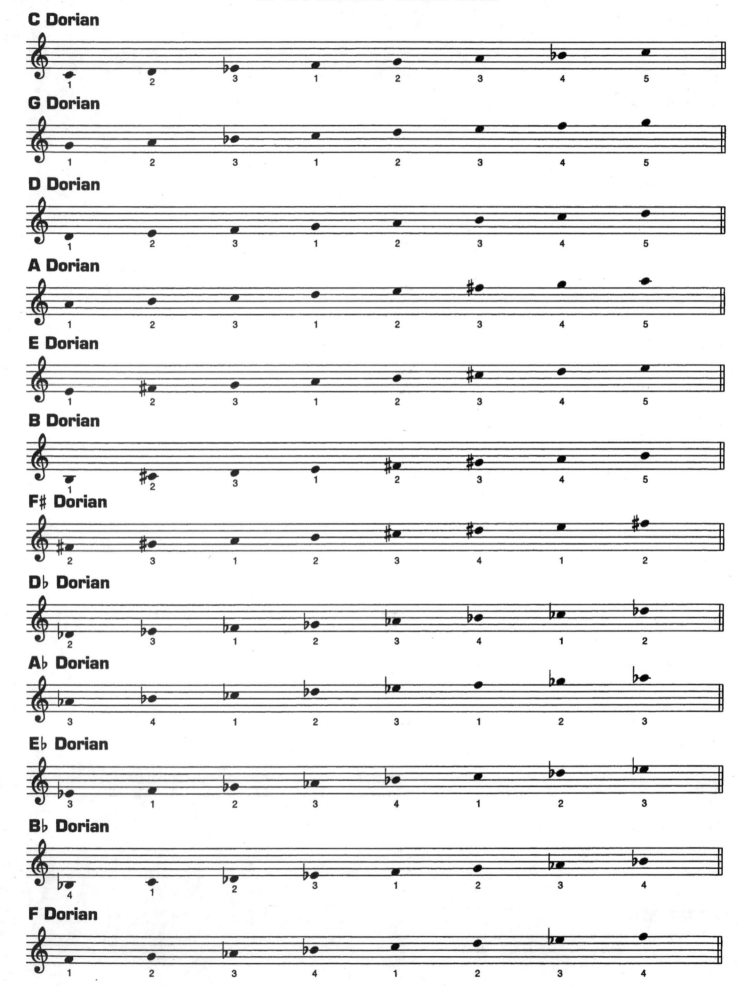